COMMUNICATION

contributors

LEROY G. AUGENSTEIN

PETER MARLER

NOAM CHOMSKY

ABRAHAM KAPLAN

ERIC H. LENNEBERG

Communication

A DISCUSSION AT THE NOBEL CONFERENCE

organized by Gustavus Adolphus College, St. Peter, Minnesota, 1969

edited by

JOHN D. ROSLANSKY

Woods Hole, Massachusetts

1969

NORTH-HOLLAND PUBLISHING COMPANY–AMSTERDAM·LONDON
FLEET ACADEMIC EDITIONS, INC. – NEW YORK

PRINTED IN THE NETHERLANDS

Editor's Acknowledgement

The lectures presented on January 8–9, 1969, during the occasion of the fifth Nobel Conference have been assembled in the present volume. Scholars from diverse disciplines have once again generously interrupted their busy lives for the benefit of interested laymen, high school and college students. In focusing their attention on the topic 'Communication', they have directed their careful concern and cooperative interests towards the unending search for knowledge and insight into relevant human problems. One can hope that the rewards derived are a matter of mutual benefit and that this represents a constructive effort to bridge both the generation and information gap of which one is constantly reminded in recent times.

As on past occasions, those of us who were privileged to visit the campus were grateful for the usual cordial welcome and the considerate attention enjoined upon us by the greater college family. Those responsible for development of the conference wish to extend their special appreciation to the Hill Family Foundation, whose interest was critical to the initiation and development of the conference series, during this their final year of support. The substantive contributions of the Arnold Ryden Foundation, Tozer Foundation, Bremer Foundation and the Board of College Education and Church Vocations of the Lutheran Church of America are again respectfully acknowledged.

We are most appreciative for the permission kindly granted by the family of Dr. Peter J. W. Debye for inclusion of the Tribute which honors his memory. Particular appreciation is extended to Dr. Raymond Fuoss of Yale University who, at the

recommendation of Dr. Theodore Shedlovsky of Rockefeller University, respectfully prepared the Tribute honoring the memory of their friend and colleague. The editor's duties were simplified by the prompt and courteous attention of participants in the preparation of necessary materials.

JOHN D. ROSLANSKY

Tribute to Peter J. W. Debye

This fifth volume of the Nobel Conference Lectures honors the memory of Peter J. W. Debye, Nobel Laureate in Chemistry in 1936 with the citation: 'for his contributions to the study of molecular structure through his investigations on dipole moments and on the diffraction of X-rays and electrons in gases'. Dedication of this symposium on Communication to Debye is especially appropriate because so much of the progress of the last half century in chemistry and physics stems from his masterly ability to communicate his ideas to the scientific world.

The award of the Nobel Prize in Chemistry to a Professor of Physics indicates the scope of Debye's interests and accomplishments, as does the sequence of his titles: Professor of Theoretical Physics (Zurich, 1911; Utrecht, 1912), Professor of Theoretical and Experimental Physics (Göttingen, 1913), Professor of Experimental Physics and Director of the Physics Laboratory (Zurich, 1920), Director of the Physics Institute (Leipzig, 1927), Professor of Physics and Director of the Kaiser Wilhelm Institute (Berlin, 1934), Professor of Chemistry (Cornell, 1940). Physical chemistry, theoretical physics, and experimental physics were all enriched by Debye's contributions.

His earliest work, some published before his doctorate in 1908, was in theoretical physics, on Foucault currents in rectangular conductors, diffraction of light by cylinders and spheres, and propagation of electromagnetic waves. His doctoral thesis dealt with the pressure of radiation on spheres of arbitrary electrical properties; available mathematical tools were inadequate for the problem so Debye created new ones by his extension of Hankel functions to argument and index of infinite order. In 1912, his theory of the specific heat of solids was published. In the same year, the theory of dielectrics, based on his concept of permanent dipoles, was presented; this was one of the three items for which he was to receive the Nobel Prize twenty-four years later. This work explained in terms or molecular parameters the temperature dependence of dielectric constants, made possible the determination of dipole moments and their correlation with molecular structure, and eventually lead to an explanation of the frequency dependence or dielectric properties.

About the same time, he became interested in X-ray diffraction in crystals (discovered in 1912 by Von Laue), and developed the theory of the temperature dependence. In the process, he invented the Debye factor which gives the intensity of the diffraction spots in terms of wave length, angle and temperature. A little later (1916), experimental work began on the scattering of X-rays from crystalline powders. The Debye–Scherrer method became one of our most powerful tools for establishing the structure of crystalline materials. Later, the theory of electron distributions in atoms was worked out in terms of the atom form factor. The structure of liquids also was studied by X-rays. Then electron scattering by gas molecules was used to investigate their structure.

The current theory of electrolytes is based on the 1923 papers of Debye and Hückel, in which the previously incomprehensible thermodynamic and transport properties of electrolytic solutions were shown to be the consequence of the long-range electrostatic forces between the ions. Many other further developments of the theory of electrolytes followed.

A fifth major field of Debye's activity was polymers. He showed that molecular weights, virial coefficients and dimensions could be determined from the angle and concentration dependence of the intensity of monochromatic light scattered by polymer solutions.

To Debye's many direct contributions to theory and experiment should be added the enormous amount of research inspired by his pioneering work in dielectrics, X-ray and electron scattering, electrolytes and polymers.

RAYMOND FUOSS
Yale University

Contents

Editor's Acknowledgement   V

Tribute to Peter J. W. Debye   VII

A little black box called the mind
LEROY G. AUGENSTEIN
Michigan State University, East Lansing, Mich.   I

Animals and man: communication and its development
PETER MARLER
The Rockefeller University, New York, N.Y.   23

Form and meaning in natural language
NOAM CHOMSKY
Massachusetts Institute of Technology, Cambridge, Mass.   63

The life of dialogue
ABRAHAM KAPLAN
University of Michigan, Ann Arbor, Mich.   87

A word between us
ERIC H. LENNEBERG
Cornell University, Ithaca, N.Y.   107

LEROY G. AUGENSTEIN

A little black box called the mind

DR. LEROY G. AUGENSTEIN *received his B.S. in 1949 from the University of Chicago, and his M.S. and Ph.D. degrees from the University of Illinois–the latter in 1956.*

Dr. Augenstein's professional experience includes an assignment with the Control Systems Labs of the University of Illinois from 1951 to 1956, followed by a two year appointment at the Brookhaven National Laboratory and repeated from 1960 to 1962. He was a member of the United States Atomic Energy Commission from 1958 to 1960. In 1960–1961 he served as the science coordinator for the United States Science Exhibit at the Seattle World's Fair. Michigan State University called him to the position of Professor and Chairman of the Department of Biophysics in 1962. In 1966 he was elected to an eight-year office on the State Board of Education in Michigan.

Constantly in demand as a lecturer, Dr. Augenstein delivers about 200 public lectures each year on various aspects of science, ethics and education. He has made numerous television programs at Michigan State University and for the three major networks.

As a writer, Dr. Augenstein served as editor for the proceedings of two international symposia on Biological Effects of Radiation *(1960, 1963) and was co-editor of the review series* Advances in Radiation Biology *published in 1963. He is the author of over 75 articles in professional journals and 25 articles on science and ethics in popular publications. His book,* Come let us Play God *was published by Harper Row this year.*

His organizational memberships include: Biophysics Society, Radiation Research Society, American Association for the Advancement of Science, and honor membership in the Sigma Xi science fraternity.

At the start of the Space Race a nagging question kept arising, 'What is going to happen when we send our astronauts out into the isolation of space for days, weeks or even months on end?' In fact, in some early experiments prospective astronauts were dumped into a spherical tank of water which was uniformly lighted, and as near body temperature as possible; the astronauts were naked and only had a helmet to supply breathing air. Alarmingly a number of the men literally went off the deep end after a very short time and would go clawing around trying desperately to get out. Since this was before the days of good tranquilizers, there was considerable difficulty in calming them down, even after they were fished out of the tank of water. The results suggested that depriving these subjects of sensory information about gravity, lighting, temperature gradients and communications from other people caused them to go berserk.

As a consequence, a number of laboratories undertook to investigate further the basic question of what happens to people in isolation. One of the simplest, and yet most rewarding experiments was run at McGill University in the Laboratory of Dr. Hebb. They simply paid students by the hour to go into an isolation room which was sound-proofed, vibration-proofed, draft-proofed, etc.; initially to minimize the input of sensory information they even had the students lie on a form-fitting, contour couch and partially immobilized their elbows so they couldn't reach up and scratch their noses or ears.

Students being the clever devils we professors know them to be would, of course, go in after a late heavy date, so they got paid for ten to twelve hours of sleep time. After they awoke, though, the fun began. Remember, there were no pencils or papers, no books or anything else – just they and the four walls. Within a few hours, almost everyone of the subjects tried some form of clever trick to get the people on the outside to communicate with them without themselves turning the doorknob to open the door because that stopped the payment. When they gave the students a microphone so they could speak out (but there was no loudspeaker coming back in) they produced a wide variety of tales to try to get people on the outside to communicate with them. When the experimenters realized how much the students craved communication, they asked themselves the obvious question, 'What will they accept?' Accordingly they put a switch in the room so that everytime the student pushed the button he got a long, prerecorded, very obnoxious commercial: once it was started it had to play through to the end.

Most of the students normally stayed in about two days during which they were awake about 30 hours. Some of them played these things over and over again as many as 50 times. Considering how bad the commercials were, the experimenters wondered whether they were listening to this junk or just pushing the button to break the monotony.

In a third part of the experiment they replaced the commercial with an even longer argument about why they should believe in flying saucers. For this part they preselected people who didn't believe in flying saucers or any of the supernatural. Again, the recordings were played over and over again. Let me emphasize the door was unlocked so that at any time the students could walk out and furthermore, this was self-imposed for payment of less than $ 1.00 per hour. When these students came out they not only believed in flying saucers, but retained this belief for quite a long period of time and in many cases tried to convert their roommates.

Clearly this raises fantastic possibilities. This seems to indicate that in a situation of sensory deprivation, a person is willing to erase information and write in new, or at least to overwrite information. Clearly, this technique can be used for tremendous good or tremendous bad. If a small, select group used it for political control we know what would happen – the communists have already demonstrated this. But on the good side of the coin, how wonderful it would be if we could bring psychotic individuals into such a situation and retrieve them to full productive life; 50 percent of our hospital beds right now are occupied by mental patients.

This is where the situation stood five years ago, and where it stands today. The reason is that no one has the courage – or perhaps the arrogance – to see how far this can be pushed because to really test these techniques would require taking some human being apart psychologically and putting him back together. In fact, many people who are concerned in this area argue that we do not have the right to mess around with someone else's beliefs, that those are his and his concern alone. Their argument is that we can intervene legitimately only when beliefs lead him to behavior which causes problems for others in society.

But there have been tremendous strides in manipulating behavior also. Some of the striking results have been obtained by Dr. Lovaas in Los Angeles. Autistic children are perhaps some of the most withdrawn individuals that we can possibly encounter. Not only do these youngsters not respond to normal communication, but many are so self-destructive that they must be placed in a strait jacket to protect themselves. However, in many cases even a strait jacket isn't enough, since unless their head is totally immobilized, they will take bites out of their shoulders, etc. To illustrate how potent and effective this can be, we can relate the example of one youngster who had been almost totally immobilized for 7 out of his 11 years. Any time they turned him loose he would chew on his shoulder. When Lovaas had him stripped and turned loose in his treatment room, he immediately turned his head to take a bite out of his shoulder at which point he was given a real jolt of electric current from a cattle prod. Stunned, he looked around bewildered for a few seconds but then turned toward his other shoulder, at which point he was given another zap. This caused him to pause for almost a minute at which point he hesitantly turned as if to take a bite, and was given a third jolt. He never again tried to do this so long as he was in the laboratory. Next, using milder shocks to the soles of his feet from an electrified floor, they were able to get him to go and throw himself into the arms of an adult counselor to avoid this punishment. Accordingly, after a month or so he began to respond to treatment and to communicate in a meaningful way. Interestingly enough when they took him back to his previous hospital ward, he went back to his old tricks of drawing blood; he knew if he did this the nurses would pick him up and cuddle him. Thus, with their so-called 'love' they were maintaining his abnormal behavior, whereas this 'evil' cattle prod could be used to restore some semblance of normal behavior. Many other instances of various animal training techniques have been used successfully in a variety of cases.

Again, it is not known just how far these things can be pushed, but we do know they can be quite effective, for at least certain types of abnormal behavior. One big question, of course, is, how and why do these things work?

To manipulate either a person's basic concepts or his behavior requires that we get information in, that it will be stored away in his memory and then retrieved in preference to other instructions. While I can't begin to elaborate all of the details of how these various processes work there is pertinent research which gives insight into some features of each of these operations.

In my own laboratory we have really treated people like a 'little black box' or computer to find out what his capabilities are for processing information. For example, we find that when skilled typists and pianists 'play' a random score or text they have a definite capacity corresponding to the making of 20–30 yes–no decisions per second: the maximum capacity measured in any laboratory is about 50 yes–no decisions per second for people very skilled in language recognizing words in randomized lists.

Further, we know that this capacity is not imposed by a limitation on our ability to take in information. Specifically, the eye takes in information four or five times a second: the actual time required for input is only a brief 0.01–0.04 sec. If you watch someone read, you can easily observe that there are gross movements of the eyes four or five times per second. From research in other laboratories it appears that the input of information occurs during these movements and during the in-between intervals the eye is essentially motionless and re-fractory.

Information taken in during one of these brief bursts is stored away for about $^1/_4$ sec in a very short-term storage unit. It appears that a surprising amount of detail is stored away initially but the information decays in its quality very rapidly, so that eventually the eye is triggered to move again to replenish the information in the short-term bank.

Presumably while the information is stored in this short-term unit, it is processed by a computational unit which has some of the properties of a digital computer. That is, a computer reads in information and stores it away and then takes this information one piece at a time and processes it through a computational cycle. If it gets an answer, it stops and reports out. If it doesn't, it takes the next piece of information and goes through the computational cycle again and so on, until a decision is reached. Certainly the data which we currently have in our laboratory is remarkably similar in behavior – our humans arrive at a decision either now or a fixed time later or a fixed time after that. . . Apparently the time required for one computational cycle is approximately 1/30th of a second or perhaps 1/100 rather than the 1/1,000,000th as in a computer.

Once information is processed we know that it goes into a short-term memory where it remains for anywhere from 5 sec to 40 min. I'll come back in a moment to indicate that the reason for this big discrepancy is not really sloppy science, but rather some factor which we don't understand apparently determines just when the information will be transferred into our permanent memory where it remains for periods up to 100 years. Let me briefly describe some of the critical experiments which have led to these conclusions.

For about 25 years or more it has been claimed that certain kinds of mental disorders can be treated effectively by electro-convulsive shock. This is done by putting an electrode on each temple of a person and passing a sufficiently powerful surge of current through the brain so that the person is knocked un-conscious and it takes a few hours to recover.

It has been observed repeatedly that if you ask this patient the next day, 'Were the electrodes too tight?' or 'Were they cold when we put them on?' or 'Was the cot on which you were lying comfortable?' invariably the patient would say, 'What electrodes?' or 'What cot?' In fact, the patient had a lot of trouble remembering what had happened in the 30 to 40 min previous to the shock.

The same is observed in certain kinds of anesthesia. For example, when people are given ether, they can usually remember the mask being put on but have trouble remembering how they got into the operating room. These findings were interpreted as indicating that the electroshock or the anesthesia blocked the incorporation of the information from the short-term memo-ry into the long-term memory, so it was effectively erased. Some experiments with white rats also seemed to confirm this conclusion. In these experiments they took a group of rats and put them into a maze. In this case it was a fairly complicated maze with a large number of right and left turns required to get the cheese at the other end; when they let the rats practice for 15 min a day it took them about 2 weeks to learn to run through the maze with no mistakes. They then took another group of rats and let them practice for 15 min a day in the same maze, but then immediately anesthetized them; no matter how long they practiced they never really learned. However, they let another group also practice for 15 minutes a day but then waited for two hours after the training session before anesthetizing them. This group learned almost as rapidly as if they had not been anesthetized. When they tried all intervals in between, the critical time again seemed to be 30–40 min. And so many of us tentatively concluded that perhaps this was a unique storage time for memory in all types of animals.

It was necessary to critically revise the generality of this conclusion when Chorover and his group ran another simple set of experiments with white rats. In this case they put them on a wooden pedestal in a cage surrounded by an electrified floor. When the rats hopped off they, of course, received a severe shock which caused them to jump high in the air. While they were in the air, the current was turned off and the rats were then returned to their cages. If they brought them back an hour, a day, a month or a year later and put them on the pedestal they remembered. That is, they would sit there and quiver and defecate and be very unhappy, but they wouldn't jump off. This is one of the few cases of 'one-shot learning' of which I am aware. They then tried to 'erase' the learning by attaching electrodes to the ears to pass an electroconvulsive shock through the animals' brains. In order to get them to 'forget' it was necessary, however, to give the shock within a very few seconds – they couldn't wait 30 or 40 min.

For a while we thought this might indicate that the time information remains in the short-term memory before it is incorporated into the permanent memory depends upon the urgency of the information. However, there are now quite a few experiments which indicate that, in fact, information is probably not erased by such treatments, but rather is stored away under different conditions of 'retrievability'. In other words, depending upon the circumstances at the time the information is incorporated into the long-term memory it may be easy or hard to retrieve. That is, in some situations a 'red flag' is associated with the happening suggesting to the animal that it should forget this, since it may be unpleasant; whereas, if things are pleasant at the time of storage then a 'green flag' will be attached so that the animal recalls this information frequently. I use the terms 'red and green flags' because we simply don't know what mechanisms actually determine re- trievability. There is now appreciable evidence, however, that human beings do have far more stored away than they can retrieve by normal methods.

Recently clinicians have checked patients more carefully who have received electroconvulsive shock. When the doctor makes sure that something happened during the 30–40 min interval prior to the shock which had to be unique for the patient, the next day, the patient would invariably claim he couldn't remem- ber. However, if the doctor persisted, very often the patient would finally say, 'Well, if you must know, . . .' The information was there, it just had a red flag on it.

In some cases hard-to-retrieve information can be gotten out by hypnosis. However, it now appears to be fairly clear that very often we not only get what is stored there, but in addition the person who is hypnotized embellishes the story to try and please the hypnotizer. The results from other experimental operations, however, indicate that information can be stored away in great detail which cannot be retrieved by normal procedures.

A few older people get a continual shake called Parkinsonism. At least one form of this malady is caused by a malfunction in

the thalamus or switchboard region of the brain. A surgeon
dare not go in there with a scalpel, because the damage he would
do in passing through the outer layers of brain would be worse
than having the palsy itself. But if a very thin electrode is put
into the right place, a surge of current can burn out just a tiny
hole in the brain so as to give a pretty high cure rate for this
type of Parkinsonism. The important thing is that the patient
must be conscious during the operation. Thus, some surgeons
began to stimulate the brain with a very weak current – similar
to that normally found in brain cells – as they pushed the electrode through toward the thalamus. They got quite remarkable
results.

In one outstanding case a woman suddenly began to hum a
piece of music right in the middle of a conversation she was
having with some of the people in the operating room. One
of the surgeons was a cellist who recognized this as a piece
from a very obscure quartet. About an hour after the operation
he went back to the lady's room and began to hum the tune.
There was no obvious recognition, but he was persistent.
Finally she said, 'Oh, I know the name of that piece'. She told
him that twenty years before she and her husband were on a
vacation quite some distance from their hometown. They came
into a small town which she named, and checked in at the
Grand Hotel at 4:30 in the afternoon. They saw that a quartet
was playing at 7:30 p.m. at the Roxy Theater which they found
had a very bright red door, etc., etc. Later checking showed
that these and similar details were correct, even though both
the theater and hotel had burned down some 15 years before,
so there could have been no immediate refreshing of memory.
There are now about 50 instances of this kind of retrieval of
information which has been stored away which can not be gotten
out by normal means.

Similar results have been found by Penfield and Jasper
working with epileptics who have an aura (i.e., the vivid recall

of some scene or a passage of music) just prior to going into their convulsion. Accordingly, they put electrodes in various regions of the brain where they thought it might be possible to stimulate one of these auras. In approximately 1200 attempts they were able in 50 cases to place the electrode such that stimulation with a weak current started the music and caused a convulsion. If they let the patient recover and did the same thing the next day, they would get a repeat performance: the music started at the same place, played through to a specific point and then followed the convulsion. They then attempted to burn out a microscopic hole in this region to see if they could prevent the aura and thus the seizure. In many cases they were successful but in a sizeable fraction of the cases they were not. This seems to imply that we can put red flags on certain happenings, but that as we all know, in many cases we will get a recall of a particular memory through a number of different associations. Their fairly low fraction of successes indicates, however, the very great magnitude of the problems that might be involved in attempting to deliberately place red flags on certain happenings in a person's life.

Even so, the very great beginnings that have been made and the impressive group of researchers who are working in these and related areas suggest that we had better begin to consider what we want to do with this information and these capabilities, once they are developed.

In many cases we would like to be able to change green flags to red – in other words to erase some information. For example, I am sure that most people like myself were horrified three years ago at Christmas time to read about the teen-age girl in Los Angeles who, selling Christmas candy, was dragged into a house where 10 or 12 thugs raped her repeatedly. In spite of some of the best psychiatric care available she reverted to the behavior of a child with severe mental depression and retardation. Probably if we could put a red flag on the happenings of that day it would be possible to retrieve her to a normal life. The obvious problem is, once you begin to play this game who decides what is to be suppressed?

Many of us would also like to be able to alter the abnormal set of beliefs in criminals such as Caryl Chessman. The book which he wrote during the twelve or thirteen years he spent on Death Row indicated that here was an extremely sharp mind. Unfortunately, though, he liked to go down Lovers' Lane and rape the girls and kill their male escorts. If someone could have gone in and changed that set of values, again, we probably would have been able to retrieve a valuable member for society.

Assuming we can develop these techniques, though, the question becomes, who determines what new values you put into a Caryl Chessman? Should it be the prisoner himself? He or she may not be the best candidate, since after all they have gotten themselves into serious trouble. Should it be the psychiatrist? Most psychiatrists and counselors take the approach that they should get the person to understand why he is behaving abnormally and then let him choose for himself. However, for many people this may be the worst thing which can be done, because bad as their behavior may be, it may still reflect a tremendous amount of accommodation that dare not be disturbed without even more serious repercussions. Should it be the parents of a criminal? In many cases they are the reasons why the prisoner is where he or she is. Or should it be society?

Let's see a show of hands. How many of you say it should be the Caryl Chessmans? Two to five percent. How many say it should be the psychiatrists? Five to ten percent. How many say it should be society in some form or another? About twenty percent. I assume most of you are saying, then, it should be the parents? In fact, disregarding the abnormal situation of the prisoner, let me ask a much more general question, how many of you would say that by and large parents should be primarily responsible for the values that go into their children? Most hands go up.

Now suppose that we do develop the mind manipulation techniques to the point where we can put almost any values we want into a child. In other words, we are imagining that you can now raise your child permissively for as long as you can stand it, and then one day you bring him in and say, 'Okay, this is values day', and essentially program him like a computer. The great virtue of this supposed system is that you now know precisely what values have been put in this child. Assuming that it may be possible to do that, how many of you would choose to use this technique? Extremely few hands are raised.

I am a bit confused. Most of you said parents should be responsible for the values of their children, but not be deliberate about it. What are we supposed to be, sloppy parents? You chuckle, but you see the point.

What are our obligations to the youngsters we bring into this world, really? All too often people fail to realize that just procreating a life doesn't make one a parent. Unfortunately two fools in a drunken stupor can do this and do it far too often. No, to be a parent you have to play God for that child by giving it a set of values, if you are going to do the job properly. In fact, this is a role that no parent can escape. Even those who claim they won't put any values into their children are, in fact, instilling a crucial value, namely, there is no such thing as proper forms of behavior. This is an extremely important concept to put into any child. Thus, I state flatly to young people that if you are unwilling to assume the hard job of playing God for a child by giving it a proper set of values, then don't bring it into this world!

Of equal concern, how deliberate should we be in giving values to those youngsters whose parents don't do a proper job for them? No segment in society has a corner on the market of these youngsters. The largest fractional increase in the crime rate occurs in our upper middle class suburbs. Also, the hippies are not from the ghetto nor are they rebelling against what they find in the ghetto. Nevertheless, this is where we must be most concerned, since this is perhaps the biggest problem facing America today. If we don't correct this one then our country will come unstuck and we may not be able to glue it back together.

I first became aware of what happened to youngsters in the ghetto when I was at the University of Chicago in 1949 and 1950 while that area was in a tremendous state of flux. But then I moved away into upper middle class areas and tried very hard to forget. However, in 1966 when I campaigned in the Republican primary for the United States Senate and later for the Michigan State Board of Education I had enough experiences that I can no longer forget nor disregard. For example, I had a high school counselor in Detroit show me where three of his pupils 'lived'. One of these boys slept under the stairwell of an apartment building, where the people across the hall were good enough to let him in to use their bathroom in the morning. When I saw him I said to the counselor, 'Why doesn't he go home?' He said wryly, 'Home? He doesn't know what the word means. He never knew who his father was. One day when he was eight his mother left him at the neighbor's while she went shopping. The next day they received an envelope with $ 25 in it and a note which said, 'Joe and I have gone to Arizona. When we strike it rich we'll send for you'. Apparently they haven't struck it rich because the boy is now 16 and he still hasn't heard from them.' Even before the riots there were 8 to 10 thousand such youngsters in the city of Detroit alone.

Further, the McCone report on the riots in Los Angeles pointed out that many of the youngsters which they picked up in the Watts subdivision were exactly like our young man in Detroit. They had never known who Dad was and Mother put them out on the streets at the age of 8, 9, or 10. That report and others also indicate why many of these youngsters don't behave in the same way as I am used to. For example, in one of their larger housing developments, out of 336 households only 11 had a father in residence.

Values could be instilled in Operation Headstart and comparable preschool programs. Anyone who has participated in this program for any period of time will tell you that while it helps to teach these youngsters words and concepts, this is not the real benefit. Rather, the greatest thing for these youngsters is that they finally sit on someone's knee who says, 'Look, little Joe, it is important to me that you are little Joe'. As I found with one youngster for whom I served as a 'foster father' when I was going to the University of Chicago, once he was convinced I was sincere, then suddenly that little mind opened up almost like in the situation of sensory deprivation, and you basically have a blank slate on which to write. Thus, comes the critical question facing all of our society today. Should we go one step further and say, 'Look, little Joe, if you want to get along in this world you had better adopt my middle class set of values'.

How many of you would say that we should never impose our values onto someone else, and particularly, someone else's child? About 20 percent. You have just consigned that youngster to society's scrapheap, because without a set of values he or she will have no chance of competing, unless of course you are willing to completely tear our society apart and remake it so as to encompass their way of living. Further, I hope you have never worked in the ghetto, because your mere presence there is an attempt to impose a value – to tell those people there is something wrong with the way they are living.

By contrast, how many of you would argue that we have an obligation to provide these youngsters a set of values so they can compete? About 50 percent. Then I ask you, whose values? In particular, can those of you who are unwilling to raise your hands and say that you would deliberately put a set of values into your own child, ever presume to determine what values someone else's child should have?

Although this is an obviously messy dilemma to resolve, it is one that we dare not disregard. In fact, I have participated in a program which attempted to answer this question at one of the ghetto high schools in Detroit.

I and some of my colleagues are very much concerned that so few non-athlete Negro males enter college and complete it. There are two major reasons for this. First, many of these youngsters see no real value of going on to college. Secondly, they have a tremendous creditability gap – they are convinced they can't make it, no matter what. Certainly their lack of confidence is not without basis, if you look at the recent report which the Civil Rights Commission sent to the President entitled '*Racial Isolation in our Public Schools*'. For example, suppose 2 Negro children live on opposite sides of a street which divides two school districts. If one youngster goes for twelve years to a predominantly white school, his average achievement will be 11th or 12th grade. If the other goes to an essentially all-Negro school for twelve years, his average achievement will be at the 7th–9th grade level. The situation at Northern High School in Detroit last year illustrates some of the consequences of this situation. In a previous year they graduated about 250 youngsters. I was told that this was the residue of about 1,000 sophomores, and probably the residue of about 1500 youngsters at the 6th grade level. Approximately 30 of those said they were going on to college, but apparently only 9 did. No society can call itself very humane or very intelligent and allow this tremendous waste of potential to occur.

In an attempt to partially correct the situation, I and some of my colleagues developed a program in which we gave freshman-level college courses right in the high school. We hoped to show the students that professors do have only one head, and furthermore, that they are capable of coping with college material. On Saturday mornings last spring, I gave my fresh-man-level course on ethical problems arising from science. I started with 9 youngsters and finally ended up with 33 making a trip to our campus. At the end, my students laughed about the good job of brainwashing I had done on them. However, there is a very major ethical question which must be asked. I knew full well that probably half of them could never make it without extensive financial and tutoring help. Should we not have tried to convince them because 50% may fail and thus get another kick in the teeth, or did we have an obligation to do what we could so the other 50 percent would have a chance of lifting themselves up?

This illustration perhaps dramatizes as well as any the fact that anytime we communicate in a protracted and meaningful way with some other individual, values will be changed if it is a significant interaction. Thus, anyone who either brings a child into this world or who will be getting involved with someone else's child, whether it be in the ghetto or as a teacher in a grade school, high school, or university, had better very carefully re-examine their values. I certainly have re-examined mine in the last few years, and have found that many of the values which are 2000 to 6000 years old really are still pertinent today, providing they are properly reinterpreted. In fact, the more I search the more I find that the *fundamental* principles of Judaism and Christianity are still of tremendous benefit and relevance. This is true whether I am functioning in the area of mind manipulation in the ghetto, or in genetic counseling with couples who either have had or are fearful they will have a seriously defective child.

The thing which is different is the way in which these are interpreted into *operating* procedures. In this regard, as life has become more and more complex, it has become essentially impossible to write down a set of highly restrictive laws or a dogmatic set of operating procedures which will deal with each and every situation. Unfortunately, all too often people confuse fundamental moral values with operating procedures, and claim that if one of the old dogmatic rules about how to operate in a given situation no longer works, then all the values upon which that rule was based are also passé.

Those of us over 40 thus have a very important and urgent job. We must very carefully rethink and reanalyze our beliefs and practices to find out what is really bedrock principle that probably has not changed and what is operating procedures which may no longer be relevant. In many cases we hold onto old tried and true operating procedures simply because they are comfortable even after they no longer work. As a consequence, accusations by some in the younger generation about the hypocrisy of those of us in the middle-aged, middle class are sometimes correct. However, let me quickly add that I do not condemn all hypocrisy: it often serves a very useful purpose. For example, charges of hypocrisy sometimes arise simply because people set goals for themselves which being human they do not attain. Certainly, if we were to simply legitimize all behavior which we observe, then society's behavior might well quickly sink to the lowest common denominator, rather than improving.

Certainly, one of the things that both the younger and the middle-aged generations must do is to work together very carefully to see that you in the younger generation get the positive leadership you need so desperately. Up until now your demonstrations have been mainly negative since usually protests in the street must of necessity be based upon very simplistic slogans and objectives, and in many cases involve only a negative form of protest. Certainly much of the protest has been very valuable in calling attention to important defects in our society. However, now that there is adequate awareness of these defects, the youth who protested now have an obligation to go on and take positive steps to try to correct these things in a constructive way. Otherwise, they will be even more hypo-

critical than those they have criticized. Further, those who rail
out against absolutes should realize that oversimplified absolutes
are about all that can be sold in the streets and thus the complicated decisions I have been talking about here dare not be
made on the streets but rather in careful give and take.

It must be clear to everyone that this little black box we call
the mind is far more complicated than we have treated it in
our laboratory. But we in science invariably tend to make
simplifying assumptions in order to develop hypotheses which
can be tested: in most cases this is the only way we can proceed
in a rigorous way. Nevertheless, although I am aware of the
reservations which must be attached to conclusions based upon
a simplified model or analysis, I know that in the not too distant
future we will begin to unravel more and more of the complexity
of the mind and thus will learn how to control it to an even
greater extent for better or for worse. It is this which I want
to leave with you. While I or any other speaker at this symposium
may be quite wrong in our conclusions about how some particular function of the mind operates, or how communication
proceeds, the consequences of how to control and manipulate
the mind – and, in fact, to control and manipulate communication – will have the same implications I have indicated here
independent of how they work or why they work.

It is these implications and consequences that we dare not
disregard since the mind is a sanctuary for many things. Thus,
the techniques described here, or others which will come along
to replace them, can be used properly to attack and destroy
the last sanctuary of ignorance, incompetence and inequality.

In this regard, I am sure Alfred Nobel would have approved
of Longfellow's lines in *The Arsenal at Springfield:*

> Were half the power that fills the world with terror,
> Were half the wealth, bestowed on camps and courts,
> Given to redeem the human mind from error,
> There were no need of arsenals or forts.

To the contrary, if our new scientific information and techniques are misused, they will almost certainly destroy the last sanctuary of integrity and individuality. Thus, the real question we must consider and decide quickly is just who shall be given the responsibility for controlling these little black boxes which we call our minds.

Suggested auxiliary reading

Come let us play God, L. Augenstein. Harper Row (1969).
Control of the mind, S. M. Farber and R. H. L. Wilson, eds. McGraw Hill.
The neurosciences – a study program, T. Melnechuck and F. O. Schmitt, eds. Rockefeller University Press (1967).

PETER MARLER

Animals and man:
Communication and its development

DR. PETER MARLER *was born in England and his first degrees were in botany, at University College, in the University of London. While engaged in field research for a Ph.D. in botany, he became interested in the biological significance of birdsong. After a year with the Nature Concervancy in Scotland, working to establish reserves, he returned to graduate work under Dr. W. H. Thorpe at the University of Cambridge to begin study of the behavior of birds, which earned him a second Ph.D. in zoology.*

After two years as a research fellow at Jesus College at Cambridge, he moved to the University of California to develop a teaching and research program, at Berkeley, in animal behavior. He remained there until he moved to the Rockefeller University in 1966 as a professor participating in the new program in behavioral sciences as a member of the new Institute for Research in Animal Behavior, operated jointly with the New York Zoological Society.

Currently president of the Animal Behavior Society, he is active in the affairs of a number of scientific societies. He has served on advisory panels for the National Institute of Health, National Institute of Mental Health, and the National Institute for Child Development.

His research interests have ranged widely over the subject of communication in animals. A recent book on Mechanisms of Animal Behavior, *written jointly with Dr. W. H. Hamilton at the University of California, Davis, has become a standard text in advanced courses in this subject. A fruitful association with anthropologists has led to field work in Africa on the behavior of nonhuman primates, most recently the chimpanzee, and he maintains this interest in conjunction with a research program on the vocalizations of birds.*

In deliberating over the title, I was tempted to exclude communication in man. My temptation was provoked because the notion that animal and human communication can be discussed in similar terms seems nonsensical and even offensive to many people. I see no point in encouraging prejudices against what I have to say even before I have begun. If it were more customary to extend our conception of human communication to include not only the spoken and written words, but also communication by intonation or by gesture and expression, then most people would agree that there is common ground that can be fruitfully explored. But our language is often thought of as a thing apart, perhaps in some sense demeaned by propositions that we can discover something similar in animals. I do not wish to confront this problem directly. My profession is that of a zoologist and my prime interest is in understanding how animals behave and why, communication being one aspect of their behavior. This will be the main subject of my talk, I will from time to time suggest how some comparisons with human language might be made. Whether animal studies will throw light on how and why human language evolved, and why it did not evolve in any other organism than ourselves, I will leave you to decide.

To emphasize that my primary interest is in problems initially quite remote from human language, I would like to start with some remarks about communication in insects. I shall postpone any attempt to define what I mean by communication in the hope that this will become clear from my examples. A simple case which has been the subject of elegant investigation is found among the grasshoppers and crickets, many of which produce sounds that can be shown to function in social communication (Walker 1957; Alexander 1962, 1968).

In favorable localities in the southeastern United States one can hear as many as 20 different species of tree crickets producing sounds at the same time. Although both male and female can produce some sounds the most conspicuous contribution to the din of a summer's evening comes from what is described as the calling song of the males, which serves the communicative function in these tree crickets of attracting females to males when both are ready for mating. This attractiveness is readily demonstrated experimentally as Dr. Thomas Walker has shown. A cage some three feet long is fitted with loudspeakers at each end, and a reproductive female is released in the center. One loudspeaker transmits recordings of songs of a male of her own species, the other songs of another species. She will quite reliably move towards the song of her own kind. This song functions, then, in reproductive isolation of the species and such a function carries certain requirements. If a female were to respond indiscriminately to the songs of any males they heard, time would be wasted and reproduction would be ineffective, for hybrids would probably be poorly adapted or infertile, if indeed they ever developed into adult form. Clearly a mechanism is required to restrict her choice to the sounds of her species.

Investigation reveals that males of each species have a particular pulse rate in their song, and it is to this rate that the female responds. Thus, the basic situation is simple, but there are some further refinements. Tree crickets are of course, cold blooded, and the rate of many of their metabolic processes is a function of temperature. The pulse rate in the song changes with temperature, and in some species the relationship is so regular that you can tell the air temperature by counting the pulse rate, hence the name that some species have earned of 'thermometer crickets'. The changes in rate with temperature are quite drastic, and you might think that this would throw a female seeking a mate into hopeless confusion. In fact, the physiological mechanism which determines her responsiveness changes with temperature in a fashion parallel to the change in the male's song pulse rate, thus avoiding confusion.

One might ask, how you can be sure that the pulse rate is the only character to which females are responding? The quality of the individual syllables or pulses certainly sounds different to our ears in some species, and it would seem reasonable to suppose that the crickets themselves would be even more sensitive to subtle characteristics such as this. An artificial song can be generated by audio-oscillators. The females respond to this irrespective of the pulse structure, as long as the rate is normal. The most clever way to demonstrate the irrelevance of variations in pulse structure however, exploits the temperature dependence of the pulse rate.

Suppose that the male of a given species, species A, normally sings with a pulse rate of 50 pulses per sec at 70 °F. We can take males of another species, species B, whose pulse rate is normally slower than this, and warm him up until his pulse rate is also 50 per sec. This can be recorded and now played to a female of species A at 70 °F. She will respond perfectly normally, even though the pulse structure is different from that characteristic of her species.

This example of the tree crickets illustrates a number of points that are important to a zoologist in trying to characterize communication in animals. I shall try to do this largely within the framework proposed by the distinguished linguist at Cornell University, Dr. Charles Hockett, who has done more than anyone to define the very basic characteristics of human language, or design features as he calls them, in terms which might conceivably allow one to determine their presence or absence in animals, thus circumventing questions about intention and motive which were for a long time a stumbling block to comparative study of communication. This is Charles Hockett's list of the basic design features of language (Hockett and Altmann 1968).

DF1. Vocal-auditory channel.
DF2. Broadcast transmission and directional reception.
DF3. Rapid fading. (The sound of speech does not hover in the air.)
DF4. Interchangeability. (Adult members of any speech community are interchangeably transmitters and receivers of linguistic signals.)
DF5. Complete feedback. (The speaker hears everything relevant of what he says.)
DF6. Specialization. (The direct-energetic consequences of linguistic signals are biologically unimportant; only the triggering consequences are important.)
DF7. Semanticity. (Linguistic signals function to correlate and organize the life of a community because there are associative ties between signal elements and features in the world; in short, some linguistic forms have denotations.)
DF8. Arbitrariness. (The relation between a meaningful element in a language and its denotation is independent of any physical or geometrical resemblance between the two.)
DF9. Discreteness. (The possible messages in any language constitute a discrete repertoire rather than a continuous one.)
DF10. Displacement. (We can talk about things that are remote in time, space, or both from the site of the communicative transaction.)
DF11. Openness. (New linguistic messages are coined freely and easily, and in context, are usually understood.)
DF12. Tradition. (The conventions of any one human language are passed down by teaching and learning, not through the germ plasm.)
DF13. Duality of patterning. (Every language has a patterning in terms of arbitrary but stable meaningless signal-elements and also a patterning in terms of minimum meaningful arrangements of those elements.)
DF14. Prevarication. (We can say things that are false or meaningless.)
DF15. Reflexiveness. (In a language, we can communicate about the very system in which we are communicating.)
DF16. Learnability. (A speaker of a language can learn another language.)

The aim here is to try to set down the most elementary features that characterize human language, thus setting the stage for the investigation of their presence or absence in other organisms (Hockett 1963; Hockett and Altmann 1968). I have some reservations which I have expressed elsewhere about using these design features as a guide for the analysis of the vital features of animal communication systems (Marler 1967). But their value in comparing animal communication and human language cannot be questioned, even though their elementary nature may fail to do justice to many other universal features of our language. In what follows I shall concentrate only on the features which I regard as most important. To take a simple example first, one of the most elementary properties is what Hockett calls specialization. Are the signals merely incidental outcomes of other ongoing activities? Do they achieve an effect merely by their physical impact on other animals, or do they have some more sophisticated triggering effect? In other words can one see evidence of specialization for the function of communication? This is clearly evident in the sound production of leaf crickets, and similar evidence can be found throughout the animal kingdom. This feature is widespread among animals.

Another criterion is arbitrariness, pointing out that the relationship between a signal and its referent should be independent of any physical relationship between the two. The association between the word cup and its denotation in the environment is an arbitrary one. Similarly the differences between species songs in the crickets is essentially an arbitrary one. There is no a priori reason for thinking that one species had to have a higher pulse rate than another at a given temperature. To take another example, closer to Hockett's sense of arbitrariness, the form of alarm signals that some crickets may give when suddenly disturbed, bears no formal relationship to the cause of danger – the association is an arbitrary one.

A third criterion is discreteness. The possible messages in the language should constitute a discrete repertoire rather than a continuous one. Study of the song and other sounds in the

repertoire of crickets suggests that this condition is also satisfied.

Various other design features are obviously lacking in
crickets. For example, there is the question of tradition. The
differences between the conventions of any one human language
and another are passed down by learning and are not genetically
inherited. One can show that crickets which have been deafened
by removing the forelegs on which the hearing organs are
placed before they have ever produced any sound, still develop
normal sound patterns. Thus although crickets can hear, and
are responsive to what they hear, learning is not necessary for
normal development of their sound. When we come to consider
more species, we shall find that this criterion, which the crickets
do not fulfill, is satisfied by other animals, but that other elements among the basic design features of human language are
absent. And this, as Hockett has indicated, is the point that
will emerge from this survey. All, or almost all, of the basic
features of human language are known from at least one other
animal group. But nowhere else do they all coincide, with the
particular concatenation of features that permitted the explosive
development of human language.

From the viewpoint of the zoologist rather than the linguist,
the tree cricket example also draws our attention to the great
importance of understanding the particular sensory world in
which an animal lives before we can comprehend how its
members communicate with one another. Take for example
the apparent irrelevance of the structure of the pulses from
which the tree cricket songs are composed. Is this something
that the crickets perceive but simply ignore? Although these
animals can hear, they do so in a very different way from us,
and one can show that variations of pitch and timbre are
virtually imperceptible to them. Their ears are so constructed
as to be especially responsive to variations in loudness, but
pitch means little or nothing to them. Thus it is not surprising

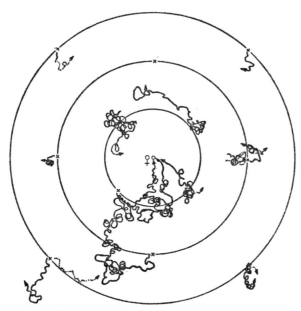

Fig. 1. The male silkworm moth, *Bombyx mori*, may be unable to find a female even when she is only a meter away if there is no moving air. The concentric circles are one meter apart. Tracks of the males are for one-hour periods. After Schwinck (1954).

that pulse structure in the calling song is irrelevant to them.

To take another example, some animals are much more responsive than we are to the chemical characteristics of the environment in which they live, and this sensitivity is also exploited in their social communication. Recent studies have revealed a wealth of so-called pheromones, chemical signals that are used for purposes of communication, in both inverte-brate and vertebrate animals (Wilson 1968). A species may possess a repertoire of different signals, produced by various glands on the body, transmitted in different ways and with different diffusion characteristics, serving to lay trails, induce

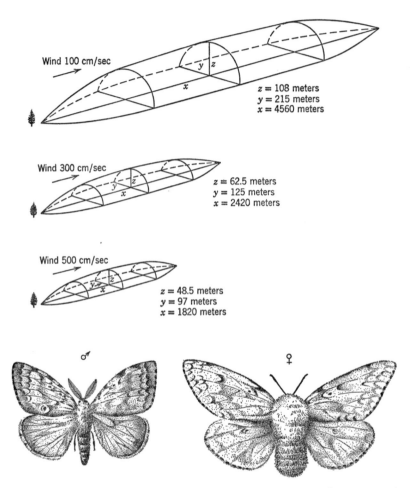

Wind 100 cm/sec

z = 108 meters
y = 215 meters
x = 4560 meters

Wind 300 cm/sec

z = 62.5 meters
y = 125 meters
x = 2420 meters

Wind 500 cm/sec

z = 48.5 meters
y = 97 meters
x = 1820 meters

Fig. 2. The distance and area from which female gypsy moths can recruit males with their sex attractant chemical, decreasing with increasing wind speed, may be calculated by reference to gas diffusion laws and analysis of turbulence. Note the male's large antennae. After Wilson and Bossert (1963).

mating, encourage aggregations for resting, to disseminate alarm, to permit recognition of individuals and groups, and to attract others to a food source. Once again, it is particularly important to understand the characteristics of a given modality if signal function is to be understood.

Consider for example the elementary function of enabling one animal to find another, a very widespread function for communication signals of animals. With visual signals this is very easy. It is barely possible for an animal to perceive a visual signal without getting some idea of the position of the source in space. With sound it is a little more difficult, as we shall discuss in a moment. With chemical signals the complications are even greater. A female moth may be able to attract a male of her species from distances as great as a mile, by means of the sex pheromone that she emits. However, this is only possible under very special conditions. If the chemical stimulus is diffusing out from a point source in a still medium, air in this case, a diffusion gradient will result. This gradient is the only clue that an animal can use in locating the source as long as the medium remains still. To be detected, such a gradient must be fairly steep, and the effect is to make it impossible for a male to locate a female under these conditions at a distance greater than a meter or two (Schwinck 1954; Fig. 1). However, if the wind is blowing, then the male can determine the direction of the wind and fly against it (Fig. 2). In this way he is able to approach the female from much greater distances (Wilson and Bossert 1963). But clearly special conditions are required, and in fact females will restrict the emission of their scent to times when the atmospheric conditions are appropriate. These problems would not arise with a visual signal, but of course it would be difficult for moths to create visual signals that could be perceived by others at these great distances. This would have to take place in daylight, whereas pheromones are equally efficient in darkness. In animal communication we often find this kind of compromise between the advantages and disadvantages of different sensory modalities.

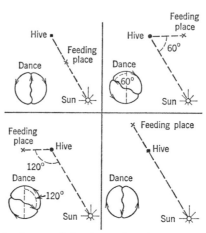

Fig. 3. The waggle dance of the honeybee is performed on the vertical face of combs inside the dark hive. The direction of the waggle run across the diameter of the circle conveys the direction of the food discovery. In the hive the direction is relative to the vertical, in flight relative to the sun. Thus a following bee must transpose the angle of the dance to the vertical to an angle relative to the sun when it sets out to locate the discovery that the scout has announced. After Von Frisch (1967).

An important design feature in Hockett's list is semanticity. To the extent that communication signals correspond with things in the external world, that is to say to the extent that they may have a referent of some kind, so they can be said to have a semantic property, as a name for an object does. One of the best examples from the animal kingdom again comes from lower animals in Karl Von Frisch's studies of the dancing behavior of the honeybee (Von Frisch 1967). Scout bees which discover a rich food source at a distance from the hive will return and communicate the distance and direction of the source to other workers within the hive which may then follow the instructions, and begin to exploit the source themselves. Communication is achieved by dancing behavior that the scouts perform within the dark hive on the vertical face of the comb.

They perform a waggle dance in the form of a figure eight. The line of the waggle run with respect to the vertical corresponds to the course that other workers must take with respect to the sun if the source is to be found (Fig. 3). The rate of the dancing communicates the distance of the source, the slower the pace, the further the distance. Here the form of the signalling behavior has a very specific semantic referent in the external environment.

There are other design features also illustrated by this dancing behavior. For example Hockett rightly attaches importance to the feature of displacement, which requires signalling about things that are remote in time and space from the site of actual communication. The honeybee waggle dance satisfies both of these criteria. There is a necessary delay between finding a food source and communicating about it subsequently within the hive. In fact, observations made during the night when the bees are normally inactive reveals an occasional insomniac who is still dancing to a food source which he discovered hours before during daylight.

Somewhat related to displacement is the phenomenon which Bronowski (1967) calls 'separation of effect'. By using this term he seeks to point out that 'animals do not separate the emotional charge which surrounds the message from its content of instruction'. The occurrence of displacement is greatly facilitated when this separation is accomplished. Our language can carry emotional content, but we are capable of separating the emotive content of words from their symbolic content (Ogden and Richards 1923). Although there are technical difficulties in making this same distinction in animal communication (Marler 1967) it seems clear that the transition to language requires some release from the association of signals with particular, strong, and self-sustaining emotional states. It is of the essence of language that we can discourse about dangers without necessarily being fearful at that moment. Animals do this much less often, though there is one pattern of animal behavior in which this dissociation of signals from their customarily associated emotion is common and even diagnostic, namely play behavior. A feature of much signalling behavior in social play, for example, is the frequent reversal of roles, with a rapidity which the inertial properties of the normal emotional physiological substrates would not permit. One could in fact strike a number of parallels between animal play and the babbling stage of speech development in children.

At the same time, the importance of emotional concomitants in animal signalling should not be exaggerated. In drawing attention to them we are indicating that there are often physiological correlates of the type we usually associate with emotion, often autonomic in nature. But the utterance or writing of a word also has physiological correlates and they are sometimes of an involuntarily emotional nature, as every psychoanalyst knows. Even when they are not, physiological mechanisms are still involved. Thus a difference between animals and man may exist in the kind of physiological states associated with signalling behavior, but there seems every reason to regard it as a difference in degree rather than in kind.

Another feature of interest is openness, the capacity to coin new messages which are understood. The honeybee can reasonably be supposed to communicate the direction of a food source say due west of the hive, the first time it encounters that particular direction. In principle, this is like a child responding properly to the first exposure to a recombination of familiar words in a new sentence. It will be obvious that the limitations here are quite severe ones, stemming partly from the continuous rather than discrete nature of the representations of direction in the bee dance. The combination of openness with discrete signals is the more interesting case, and this, so far as I know, is rarely if ever found among wild animals.

Another point, which is not brought out so clearly by Hoc-

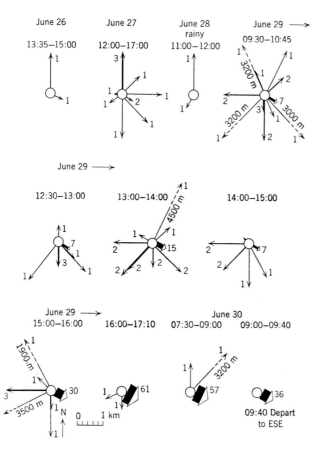

Fig. 4. The dances of scout bees on a swarm indicating the location of new nest sites they have discovered. The direction and length of the arrows indicate the direction and distance of the sites; the numbers of dances in each direction are shown and are also represented by the width of the arrows. The final site agreed on was 350 m east-southeast of the swarm. After Lindauer (1961).

kett's design features, is the importance of the context of a communicating signal. The meaning of a word may be fundamentally affected by the other words associated with it. Similarly with the bee dance, which can be used to communicate the distance and direction not only of food, but also of water, resin, and of new nesting places. The latter function is served by dancing which takes place on the surface of a swarm of bees which has left the hive, with the queen in its center, and is hanging say, on a branch of a tree. Scouts will investigate various possible sites, and indicate the quality of the site by the persistence with which they dance. A strong dancer can persuade a weak one to join him and in this way unanimity is gradually achieved and the swarm then moves off to the best site (Lindauer 1961; Fig. 4). The dancing here is identical in form with that used to indicate food, only the context being different. Similarly with dancing in the hive, the dancer often exchanges with members of its audience the contents of its crop, which may be nectar, water or resin. According to the current shortages in the hive, the audience will respond appropriately.

Remarkable though it is, the dancing of bees lacks several of the Hockett design features, notably that of traditional transmission. The honeybee needs no example from older workers to perform the waggle dance. Lindauer demonstrated this directly by removing all older bees from a colony and then studying the behavior of those that were newly emerging. Reared in isolation from adults, they came home with food they had collected and danced normally, vivaciously as Karl Von Frisch puts it, and with success. The reception and under-standing of the information however needs some practice. Initially young bees are somewhat clumsy as dance followers.

This brings up the final comment on bee dancing, that it is often exceptionally difficult to discover just how an act of communication transmits information to other individuals, or even which of the possible sensory modalities is involved. With the bee dance, we are still uncertain how this is done. The hive is dark and the audience clusters around the dancer, apparently seeking to maintain contact by their antennae. They may respond directly to the dancing bee by touch. However there is also a sound generated during dancing, a series of short buzzes of constant pitch (Esch 1961a, 1961b; Wenner 1962). The duration of the train of buzzes varies with the tempo of the dance and thus with the distance of the source and it may be that the audience responds to this. They are not normally responsive to air-transmitted sound, and we have to assume that if they do respond to it, they sense it by conduction through the comb. Only when someone persuades bees to respond readily to a completely artificial dancer, with the various characteristics of the dance varied independently, will the answer to this question be known, attempts so far having met with only limited success. As always with successful scientific projects, study of the bee dance also poses as many new questions as it solves.

No animal group exploits sounds as a medium for communication more extensively than birds, and it would be possible to illustrate many of the points that we have discussed in insect communication just as well with members of this group. Like many insects, birds have a large repertoire of distinct sounds serving a variety of functions (Fig. 5). As in insects, we often see some evidence that the special function a call serves, has led to the evolution of a particular kind of sound. Let me give just one example that concerns alarm calls. I have touched already on the great importance for many animals of the locatability of a given signal. Sounds are certainly easier to locate under most conditions than the source of a chemical signal. But there can be complications.

Generally speaking, vertebrates rely on a comparison between stimulation at the two ears for sound localization. We are fairly typical in this respect, relying on comparisons between intensity at the two ears, phase at the two ears, and time of arrival. Thus we will locate the source of sound to the right if we perceive the sound as arriving at the right ear first, if the

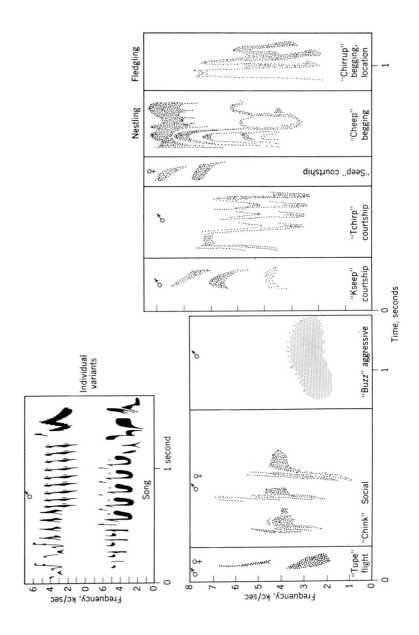

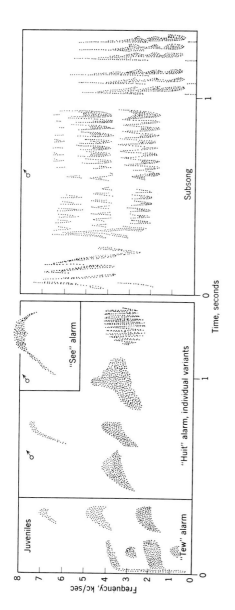

Fig.5. Tracings of sound spectrograms of the complete vocal repertoire of vocalizations of the ♀ European chaffinch, *Fringilla coelebs*. There are fourteen basic sound patterns, one of which is not shown, a squeal given when birds are taken by a predator. Some are stereotyped, and others such as the 'chink' are graded according to the context. Individual differences occur in male song patterns and the 'huit' alarm call. The sound spectrograms were made with a 300 cycle band-pass filter.

sound is louder at the right ear or if the phase at the right ear is in advance of that at the left ear. Obviously then the easiest sound to locate will be one which provides clues for all of these methods. Localization by intensity differences is most efficient with high frequency sounds because the sound shadow cast by the head only becomes appreciable when the wave length of the sound is shorter than the dimensions of the head. Low frequency sounds, with long wave lengths, simply go around the head and stimulate the far ear as much as they do the near one. So high frequencies are needed. Phase difference on the other hand is most reliable for sound location with low frequency sounds because the cue becomes ambiguous when the wave length is shorter than the distance between the two ears. Finally the method of time difference requires an abrupt onset or termination or some discontinuity in the sound, the precise time of which can be compared at the two ears.

We can design a sound which provides cues for all of these methods and the idea would be something like a sequence of click sounds, sounds with a wide range of frequencies present, low and high, and repetitive with clear, sharp discontinuities. In varying degrees a great many of the sounds used by vertebrates in social communication have some or all of these characteristics. However there are some circumstances in which locatability of a sound source is not required, and might even be a considerable disadvantage. Many birds will emit alarm calls in the presence of predators, say when a hawk is flying over. Here we could imagine a considerable advantage accruing from a sound which would be audible to other birds, and thus would disseminate alarm without at the same time giving too many clues to the hunting hawk as to where it should strike.

One can in fact design a sound which minimizes these clues. The ideal is a sound which is pitched somewhere above the maximal value at which phase difference location is possible but below the optimal for intensity differences. This sound would also lack any discontinuities, consisting ideally of a simple tone which would fade in and then fade out again without an abrupt start or finish. This is precisely the form taken by the alarm calls which a number of small birds give in the presence of a flying hawk. The 'see' alarm call of the male chaffinch is an example (Fig. 5). Several species living together may have a similar call, thus bestowing another advantage by maximizing the chances of interspecific communication. If species living together are endangered by the same predator they have nothing to lose by using a similar type of alarm call. The requirement for species specificity which we emphasized in the discussion of calling songs in the tree crickets, sounds used in reproductive isolation, is not a universal one. In some circumstances species specificity may be irrelevant, or even a positive disadvantage.

How do birds fit into Hockett's list of design features? One criterion which is otherwise absent from other animal groups apart from man, concerns the traditional transmission of the signalling behavior. If one were broaching a comparative study of vocal learning, or more strictly, of vocal imitation, it might seem logical to explore the abilities of monkeys and apes in this regard. Although chimpanzees and an orangutan have been taught to utter two or three words of human speech (Kellogg 1968), the parallel with speech acquisition is probably remote. Conditioning experiments with some other animals have tended to confirm the psychologists' impression that animal vocalizations are refractory to effects of learning as compared with other types of behavior. But there is a body of work coming not from psychology but from zoology, that argues otherwise.

We can explore this question by raising birds in social isolation, away from their own kind, to see whether this has any effect on the development of their signalling behavior. With some birds, we see little or no effect. The entire repertoire may develop normally in individuals raised in social isolation.

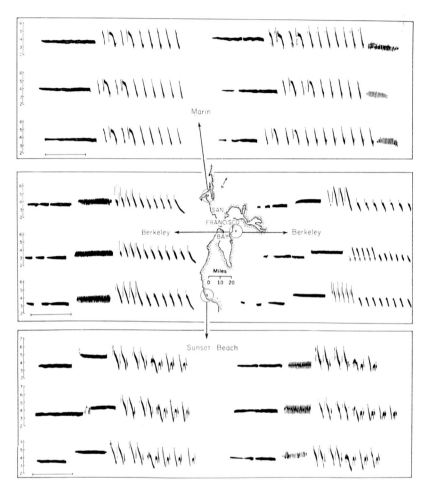

Fig. 6. Sound spectrograms illustrating dialects in the songs of eighteen male white-crowned sparrows from three localities in the San Francisco Bay area. The detailed syllabic structure of the second part of the song varies little within an area but is consistently different between populations. The introductory or terminal whistles and vibrati show more individual variability. The time marker indicates 0.5 sec and the vertical scale is marked in kHz per sec.

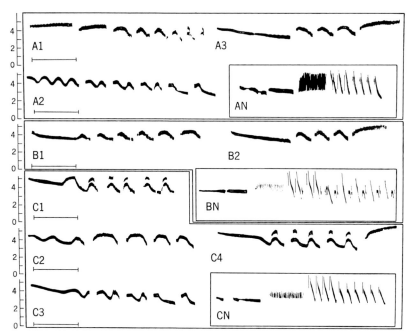

Fig. 7. Songs of nine males from three areas raised together in group isolation. A1 to A3, songs of individuals born at Inspiration Point, 3 km northeast of Berkeley; B1 and B2, songs of individuals born at Sunset Beach; C1 to C4, songs of individuals born in Berkeley. The inserts (AN, BN and CN) show the home dialects of each group.

There are other bird species however in which drastic abnormalities appear under these conditions, just as in a child which grows up in an abnormal social environment. We have studied several such cases with some care, and I would like to describe the situation briefly in one of them, the white-crowned sparrow in central California.

The natural song of males of this species varies from place to place, in the manner of local speech dialects (Fig. 6). If young birds are taken from the nest and raised in either individual or

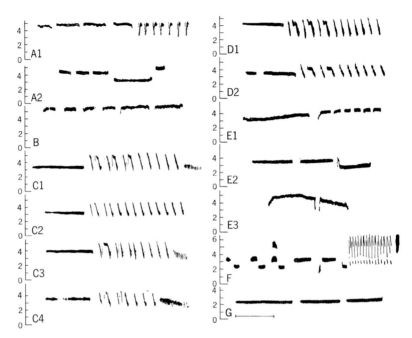

Fig. 8. Songs of twelve males raised under various experimental conditions. A1 and A2, birds raised in individual isolation; B, male from Sunset Beach trained with Marin song from the 3rd to the 8th day of age; C1 to C4, Marin birds brought into the laboratory at the age of 30 to 100 days; C1, untrained; C2 to C4, trained with Sunset Beach songs; C2 at about 100 days of age; C3 at 200 days; C4 at 300 days; D1, bird from Sunset Beach trained with Marin white-crowned sparrow song and a Harris's sparrow song (see G) from the age of 35 to 56 days; D2, Marin bird trained with Marin white-crowned sparrow song and a song-sparrow song (see F) from the age of 6 to 28 days; E1 to E3, two birds from Sunset Beach and one from Berkeley trained with song-sparrow song from the age of 7 to 28 days; F, a song-sparrow training song for D2 and E1 to E3; G, a Harris's sparrow training song for D1.

group isolation, they develop song patterns which lack the characteristics of the local dialect, and are also sufficiently abnormal to fall quite outside the class of natural patterns for the birds in their area (Fig. 7). If instead of bringing the birds into the laboratory when they are very young, we bring them in a few weeks after the time of fledging, going out and catching them with nets, then placing them in soundproof chambers, the song now develops normally, and they display the characteristics of the particular local dialect from which they came.

Experiments show that if nestlings are brought in and then given recordings of a local dialect of normal white-crowned sparrow song to listen to each day for three weeks, during the period from about 10 days after hatching to roughly 50 days of life, they subsequently develop a normal pattern of singing, with the dialect characteristics of the model to which they were exposed (Fig. 8). A bird can be taught the dialect of an area different from that where it was born. Thus the details of singing behavior are normally learned. At a very elementary level there is thus correspondence with one of the characteristics of language development in man. As in ourselves (Lenneberg 1967), there is a critical period for this learning. Exposure to normal song outside this period has much less effect on subsequent development.

As another parallel, a child concentrates its attention on human sounds in the process of speech development (Lewis 1936). Similarly a white-crowned sparrow confronted during the critical period with a choice between white-crowned sparrow song and recordings of another species which can be heard on its breeding grounds, say song-sparrow song, will make a choice and restrict its learning to the song of its own species. There are other parallels too in the role played by the organism's ability to hear its own voice during development. A sparrow deafened before singing develops a song pattern that is still more elementary than that of a hearing, isolated bird (Konishi 1965; Fig. 9). We infer that the young bird possesses some kind of hearing mechanism or template that ensures certain normal song traits – the pure tones of an isolated bird – provided it can

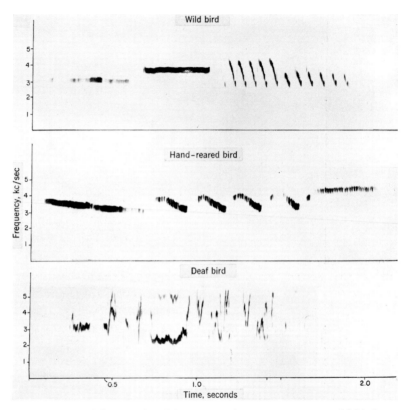

Fig. 9. Songs of three male white-crowned sparrows, one a wild bird, one a male raised in isolation from adults, and one deafened in early youth. After Konishi (1965).

use auditory feedback to match its voice to this template. This same template will suffice to focus attention during learning on sounds of its species. We hypothesize that as it listens, the template becomes more precise, now including the specifications, not only for normal song, but also for the particular dialect heard. The parallel with speech development comes in the effect of deafening at a later stage of development

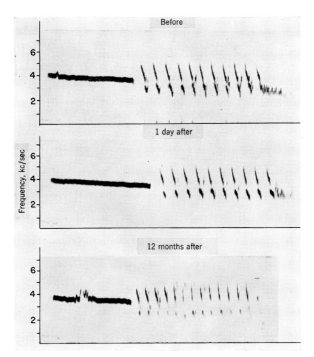

Fig. 10. Typical songs of an adult male white-crowned sparrow before deafening, one day after the operation, and a year later. After Konishi(1965).

after song development is complete. Just as a child deafened late can sustain many properties of normal speech, so a white-crowned sparrow, deafened after full song can maintain the normal patterns (Fig. 10).

Let me reiterate the parallels once more. In both child and bird, acoustical experience plays an unusually large role in shaping the structure of vocalizations. Dialects emerge in each case. Special predispositions are manifest in the learning process, concentrating attention on members of the species. Both display critical periods at which the learning most readily occurs. Audition plays the double role I have described in both bird

and man. In each case there is some evidence that the production of imitations is self-reinforcing and does not require reward by food or social approbation. Finally there are some parallels between subsong and the babbling stage of speech development (Marler, in press).

What are we to make of these parallels? Obviously they do not imply the discovery of language in birds. I believe they are manifestations of a basic set of rules that any organism engaging in vocal learning is likely to evolve if it is to function efficiently under natural conditions. Although a design feature which Hockett regards as critical for language development is satisfied, it is clear that the capacity to learn new sound patterns has a quite different consequence in birds and in ourselves. They employ it in a very specific way, actually reducing the complexity of signalling behavior within a population. These birds demonstrate traditional learning, but lack some of the other key characteristics which, coupled with the capacity to learn traditions, then make for the great expansion of our own linguistic system. In particular, these birds lack the characteristic of openness, so far as we know – the ability to constantly recombine the elements of their vocalizations to create meaningful new messages, to which others respond appropriately.

More than any other criterion it seems to me that the capacity to use a meaningful syntax is the most critical one in the transition from animal communication systems to human language. Even among primates evidence for such an ability is very hard

---

Fig. 11. Four examples of communicative gestures of wild chimpanzees that include the hand. (a) An adult female begs for food from an adult male. (b) An adult male threatens with a cuffing gesture of the hand. (c) A reassurance gesture in which two adult males, alarmed on seeing their reflections in a mirror, briefly clasp hands. (d) In the same situation an apprehensive, young-adult male places his hand in an older male's mouth for reassurance.

to find. We have been studying the signalling behavior of wild chimpanzees with this thought in mind, and it may be that combinations of sounds and gestures will prove to demonstrate openness, at a most elementary level. Perhaps the most intriguing possibility comes from the study of a captive chimpanzee.

Aware of the poor success of attempts to teach apes to speak, Drs. Allen and Beatrice Gardner, a psychologist and an ethologist respectively at the University of Nevada, sought for another method of signalling which chimpanzees might learn more readily. Field studies by Jane Van Lawick-Goodall (1968) had already demonstrated a rich repertoire of visual signals in wild chimpanzees, in which the hands often figure prominently (Fig. 11).

They argued that a chimpanzee raised away from other members of its species might conceivably be taught one of the hand sign languages used by deaf people. Bearing in mind the circumstances in which a child normally learns language they decided to raise a young chimpanzee from about 10 months of age in the confines of a fenced yard and a trailer as living quarters. They and their assistants taught themselves American Sign Language and in the presence of Washoe, as the young female chimpanzee is called, they conduct all conversation among themselves by this means. Speech is forbidden. She has opportunity to learn the sign language both in special training sessions and by observing people discoursing among themselves.

Although the project is still in progress, the results already forthcoming are exciting (Gardner and Gardner 1966–68, in press). At the time of writing, Washoe is about three and a half years old. She responds appropriately to an estimated several hundred signs. Although certain animals, especially dogs, can learn to react to many human signals, this is an impressive number. The deficits usually appear in the ability to learn to produce new signals in any large number. Washoe already shows an unprecedented facility. The following illustrate the types of gestures involved, in some of the first signs that she learned, used in a reliable fashion within thirty months of training.

Signs	Description	Context*
Come – gimme	Beckoning, with wrist or knuckles as pivot.	To persons or animals, also for objects out of reach. Often combined: 'come tickle', 'gimme sweet', etc.
More	The fingertips of the tapered hand are brought together.	Asking for continuation or repetition of activities such as swinging or tickling, for second helpings of food, etc. Also used to ask for repetition of some performance such as a somersault.
Up	The arm extends upward and the index finger may also point up.	Wants a lift to reach objects such as grapes on vine, or leaves, or wants to be placed on someone's shoulders. Also, asking to leave potty chair.
Sweet	Index or index and second fingers touch tip of wagging tongue. (Correct ASL form: use index and second fingers extended side by side.)	For dessert; occurs spontaneously at end of meal. Also, when asking for candy.
Open	The flat hands are placed side by side, palms down, then drawn apart while rotating to palms up.	At house, room, car, refrigerator, or cupboard doors, on containers such as jars, and on faucets.
Tickle	The index finger of one hand is drawn across the back of the other hand. (Adapted from ASL 'touch'.)	For tickling or for chasing games.

* This table and those which follow are copyrighted material quoted by kind permission of Gardner and Gardner.

Peter Marler

Signs	Description	Context
Go	Opposite of 'come – gimme'.	While walking hand-in-hand or riding on someone's shoulders. W. usually indicates direction desired.
Out	Curved hand grasps tapered hand; then tapered hand is withdrawn upwards.	When passing through doorways. At first, used for both 'in' and 'out'. Also when asking to be taken outdoors.
Hurry	Shaking the open hand at the wrist. (Correct ASL form: use index and second fingers extended side by side.)	Often follows signs such as 'come – gimme', 'out', 'open', 'go', particularly if there is a delay before W. is obeyed. Also, while watching her meal being prepared.
Hear – listen	Index finger touches ear.	For loud or strange sounds: bells, car horns, sonic booms, etc. Also as name for watch or clock.
Toothbrush	Using index finger as brush, rub front teeth.	When W. has finished her meal, or at other times when shown a toothbrush.
Drink	Thumb extends from fisted hand and touches mouth.	For water, formula, soda pop, etc. In last situation, often combined with 'sweet'.
Hurt	The extended index fingers are jabbed toward each other. Can be used to indicate location of pain.	To indicate cuts and bruises on herself or on others. Can be elicited by red stains on a person.
Sorry	Fisted hand clasps and unclasps at shoulder. (Correct ASL form: rub fisted hand over heart with circular motion.)	After biting someone, or when someone has been hurt in another way (not necessarily by W.). When told to apologize for mischief.

Sign	Description	Context
Funny	Tip of index finger presses nose, and W. snorts. (Correct ASL form: use index and second fingers, no snort.)	Soliciting interaction play and during games. Occasionally, when being pursued after mischief.
Please	Open hand is drawn across chest. (Correct ASL form: use fingertips and circular motion.)	Asking for objects and activities. Frequently combined: 'please go', 'Out, please', 'Please drink'.
Food – eat	Several fingertips of one hand touch mouth.	During meals and meal preparation.
Flower	The tip of the index finger touches both nostrils. (Correct ASL form: the tip of the tapered hand touches first one nostril, then the other.)	For flowers.
Cover – blanket	One hand is drawn toward self over the back of the other.	At bedtime or naptime, and on cold days, when W. wants to be taken out.
Dog	Repeated slapping on thigh.	For dogs and for barking.
You	Index finger points at chest of a person.	Indicates successive turns in games. Also, in response to questions such as: 'Who tickle?', 'Who brush?'
Napkin – bib	Fingertips wipe the mouth region.	For bib, and for washcloth. Also used for Kleenex.
In	Opposite of 'out'.	Wants to go indoors; asking a person to join her indoors.
Brush	The fisted hand rubs back of the open hand several times. (Adapted from ASL 'polish'.)	For hairbrush and when asking for brushing.
Hat	Palm pats top of head.	For hats and caps.

Sign	Description	Context
I – me	Index finger points at or touches chest.	Indicates W.'s turn, when W. and a companion share food, drink, etc. Also in phrases, such as 'I drink', and in reply to questions, such as: P.: 'Who tickle?' W.: 'You.' P.: 'Who I tickle?' W.: 'Me.'
Shoes	The fisted hands are held side-by-side and strike down on shoes or floor. (Correct ASL form: the sides of the fisted hand strike against each other.)	For shoes and boots.

There are of course many opportunities for ambiguity and error. The experimenters found it necessary to adopt criteria for the reliability of each of Washoe's signs, namely that it be judged unambiguous by several observers for a period of consecutive days of spontaneous and appropriate use. So far the following sixty-four signs have met this criterion: *1966*, come – gimme, more; *1967*, up, sweet, open, tickle, go, out, hurry, listen, toothbrush, drink, hurt, sorry, funny, please, food – eat, flower, blanket, dog, you, bib, in, brush; *1968*, hat, I – me, shoe, Roger, smell, good – thanks, Washoe, pants, clothes, cat, key, baby, clean, catch, down, look, Susan, book, oil – lotion, mine, bed, banana, hug – love, bird, pencil, Mrs. G., Greg, help, Wende, Dr. G., Naomi, fruit, comb, dirty, thread, tree, red, light, hammer, smoke (12–29–68).

One question of interest is whether Washoe restricts a sign to the particular object with which she was trained or whether she generalizes to the entire class of objects which it represents. Washoe shows every readiness to generalize freely, not only to other objects of the same class but also to photographs of them. The Gardners have complete records on movie film of Washoe sitting before a picture book and signing appropriately as the pages are turned, 'flower, baby, dog, cat' and so on. Sometimes she makes mistakes, either by confusing objects of the same general class, cat and dog for example, or by confusing signs which are similar in form, such as pants and dog. Even here there are many puzzles. Thus she never confuses key and pencil, the signs for which are so similar that they are adjacent entries in the American Sign Language dictionary.

Washoe uses signs not only by themselves but also in various combinations. The sequences are of great interest in suggesting some capacity to employ a meaningful syntax. Four signs in particular contribute to a majority of the two-sign sequences, namely 'please', 'come – gimme', 'hurry' and 'more'. The Gardners characterize these as 'emphasizers'. They have been recorded in the following two-sign combinations. The sign at the top of each column has been recorded with all those listed below it, in order of frequency of usage. In most cases both orders have been observed. Exceptions are marked with an asterisk.

Please	*Come – gimme*	*Hurry*	*More*
come – gimme	open	open	please
out	tickle	come – gimme	*drink
drink	*sweet	please	tickle
open	listen	go	gimme
go	more	drink	*sweet
tickle	out	sweet	out
sweet	drink	out	
blanket	food	food – eat	
up	toothbrush	*toothbrush	
food	*blanket	*blanket	
brush	*dog	*bib	
hat	*in		
*bib	*bib		
*flower			
*funny			
*dog			
*in			
*toothbrush			

In some other combinations of two signs, one can be said to function as a 'specifier' for the other, as in the following examples. In certain cases the usual referent is indicated in parentheses.

sweet drink
*tickle funny
go out
*go sweet (to be carried to fruit-
  bushes)
*out funny
open drink (refrigerator)
open food (refrigerator)

open out (trailer door)
*listen eat (supper bell)
*listen dog (barking)
food sweet
food drink
*listen drink (supper bell)
*there dog
*open there (faucet)

As final examples of two-sign combinations, here are some which include a name or a pronoun.

you tickle
*you drink
*you eat
*you go
*sorry, you

*I sorry
*I hear – listen
*sorry, Roger
Roger tickle
*Roger come

Washoe also uses sequences of more than two signs such as 'you go gimme', 'Roger you tickle' and 'please Roger come', all with names or pronouns. The Gardners record the following examples that include 'emphasizers'.

gimme food gimme
come tickle please
please tickle more
open please
open please hurry
come hurry please
gimme please hurry
please hurry gimme
please come hurry
gimme drink please
hurry drink please
drink please hurry
drink hurry gimme
drink gimme hurry
sweet please gimme

please food gimme
food please gimme
gimme please food
please hurry food
come open hurry
hurry come open
please open hurry
hurry open please
hurry toothbrush gimme
hurry gimme toothbrush
please hurry out
out out please out
please tickle come
come tickle hurry

Perhaps most intriguing of all is Washoe's use of the following combinations of both emphasizers and specifiers. Again the usual referent is indicated in parentheses.

please sweet drink

drink sweet please hurry
sweet drink please hurry
sweet drink please gimme
drink sweet hurry
more more more sweet drink
food out gimme (refrigerator)
in open please (close bedroom door)

out open please hurry (trailer door)

please out open hurry (trailer door)

flower please sweet
please go out
go please out

sweet drink food (meal preparations)
food drink bib (meal preparations)
hurry bib drink (meal preparations)
gimme food drink
gimme drink food
drink food hurry
please drink hurry food
please open blanket please (blanket
  cupboard)
please open please blanket (blanket
  cupboard)
please blanket out (blanket cupboard)
come, gimme sweet hurry

It is hard to avoid the impression that a primordial syntax is emerging although one notes that many of the sequences are what might be expected if Washoe was imitating not only signs but also sequences, rather than producing of her own accord combinations that are both meaningful and novel. The extent to which analogies with the syntax of language can be pressed will only be determined by further results from this most interesting project.

My conclusions with regard to the most elementary characteristics that a communication system must satisfy to qualify as language – such as the design features of Charles Hockett – is that all are probably found somewhere in the animal kingdom. None by itself represents a unique accomplishment of man. What is distinctive is the coincidence of all of them in one organism; traditional transmission so that great flexibility of signalling behavior is possible; displacement, so that we can discourse about objects and events at other times and other places than those at which they happened; openness, so that words can be recombined in new ways to create new messages with new meanings.

Yet there still remains the question, why did this happen in us and in no other species? Surely the primary causes must be ecological and social and the great increase in tool use in the Pleistocene must somehow be implicated. The emergence of a complex society became possible in which there were elaborate divisions of labor, at once sheltering some individuals from the trials of food getting or predator protection and at the same time permitting specialization for different tasks, of which tool making was probably the most important.

I suggest that animals may have been in a state at which language might have emerged many times. The reason it did not is that perhaps by itself, language offered no advantage to them. Bronowski (1967) rightly points out that many features of animal communication 'are by-products of the social psychology of animals, and reflect the general determinants which shape their communities'. It is equally valid to assert the corollary namely that a particular type of social organization is required to exploit the selective advantages of language. In this sense then it may be as important to consider social organization, as it is to take the making and using of tools into account, if we are to understand how human language evolved.

Acknowledgements

The author is most grateful to Dr. Allen Gardner and Dr. Beatrice Gardner for permission to quote from their unpublished work on teaching sign language to a chimpanzee. Original work was supported by grants from the National Science Foundation.

References

Alexander, R. D., 1962. Evolutionary change in cricket acoustical communication, *Evolution* 16, 443–467.

Alexander, R. D., 1968. Arthropods, in *Animal communication* (T. A. Sebeok, ed.), Indiana University Press, pp. 167–216.

Bronowski, J., 1967. Human and animal languages, in *To honor Roman Jakobson*, Paris, Mouton, pp. 374–394.

Esch, H., 1961a. Ein neuer Bewegungstyp im Schwanzeltanz der Bienen, *Naturwissenschaften* 40, 140–141.

Esch, H., 1961b. Über die Schallerzeugung beim Werbetanz der Honigbiene, *Z. vergl. Physiol.* 45, 1–11.

Gardner, R. A. and B. T. Gardner, 1966–68. Development of behavior in a young chimpanzee. Summaries of 1st–6th diaries. Reports mimeographed by the authors.

Gardner, R. A. and B. T. Gardner, in press. Acquisition of sign language in the chimpanzee.

Hockett, C. F., 1963. The problem of universals in language, in *Universals of language* (Joseph H. Greenberg, ed.), Cambridge, Mass., MIT Press, pp. 1–22.

Hockett, C. F. and S. A. Altmann, 1968. A note on design features, in *Animal communication* (T. A. Sebeok, ed.), Indiana University Press, pp. 61–72.

Kellogg, W. N., 1968. Communication and language in the home-raised chimpanzee, *Science* 162, 423–427.

Konishi, M., 1965. The role of auditory feedback in the control of vocalization in the white-crowned sparrow, *Zeitschrift für Tierpsychologie* 22, 770–783.

Lenneberg, E. H., 1967. *Biological foundations of language*, New York, John Wiley and Sons, Inc.

Lewis, M., 1936. *Infant speech, a study of the beginnings of language*, New York, Harcourt Brace.

Lindauer, M., 1961. *Communication among social bees*, Harvard, Mass., Harvard University Press.

Marler, P., 1967. Animal communication signals, *Science*, 157, 769–774.

Marler, P., in press. A comparative approach to vocal learning: song development in white-crowned sparrows. J. comp. physiol. Psychol.

Ogden, C. K. and I. A. Richards, 1923. *The meaning of meaning*, New York, Harcourt Brace.

Schwinck, I., 1954. Experimentelle Untersuchungen über Geruchssinn und Strömungswahrnehmung in der Orientierung bei Nachtschmetterlingen. *Z. vergl. Physiol.*, 37, 19–56.

Van Lawick-Goodall, Jane, 1968. A preliminary report on expressive movements and communication in the Gombe Stream Chimpanzees, in *Primates* (P. Jay, ed.), New York, Holt, Rinehart and Winston, pp. 313–374.

Von Frisch, K., 1967. *The dance language and orientation of bees*, Harvard, Mass., Harvard University Press.

Walker T. J., 1957. Specificity in the response of female tree crickets (Orthoptera, Gryllidae, Oecanthinae) to calling songs of the males, *Ann. Ent. Soc. Amer.* 50, 626–636.

Wenner, A. M., 1962. Sound production during the waggle dance of the honeybee, *Anim. Behav.* 10, 79–95.

Wilson, E. O., 1968. Chemical systems, in *Animal communication*, (T. A. Sebeok, ed.), Indiana University Press, pp. 75–102.

Wilson, E. O. and W. H. Bossert, 1963. Chemical communication among animals, *Recent Prog. Hormone Res.* 19, 673–716.

NOAM CHOMSKY

Form and meaning in natural language

DR. NOAM CHOMSKY *is described by* Newsweek *(August 26, 1968) as 'one of the world's foremost linguistic scientists (he has written five books and numerous papers).'*

Dr. Chomsky was born in Philadelphia, Pennsylvania. His undergraduate and graduate years were spent at the University of Pennsylvania, where he received his Ph.D. in linguistics in 1955 under the guidance of the well-known American linguist Zellig Harris. During the years 1951 and 1955, he was a Junior Fellow of the Harvard University Society of Fellows. It was at that time that he completed his doctoral dissertation, parts of which later appeared in the monograph Syntactic Structures, *published by Mouton and Company, The Hague, in 1957.*

Dr. Chomsky joined the staff of MIT and in 1961 was appointed full professor in the Department of Modern Languages and Linguistics and the Research Laboratory of Electronics. In 1966 he was appointed to the Ferrari P. Ward Professorship of Modern Languages and Linguistics.

During the years 1958 to 1959 he was in residence at the Institute for Advanced Study at Princeton. In 1962 he was appointed a Research Fellow in Cognitive Studies at Harvard. The University of California, Los Angeles, appointed him a linguistics professor in the summer of 1966, and during the fall and winter terms of 1966-1967, Dr. Chomsky was the Visiting Beckman Professor of English at the University of California, Berkeley.

Professor Chomsky was awarded an honorary degree by the University of Chicago in 1967, and by the University of London in November, 1967.

He is the author of books and articles on linguistics, philosophy, intellectual history, and contemporary issues. He is a member of the American Academy of Arts and Sciences, and numerous professional societies. In December, 1967, he was elected a Fellow of the American Association for the Advancement of Science.

When we study human language, we are approaching what some might call the 'human essence', the distinctive qualities of mind that are, so far as we know, unique to man and that are inseparable from any critical phase of human existence, personal or social. Hence the fascination of this study, and, no less, its frustration. The frustration arises from the fact that despite much progress, we remain as incapable as ever before of coming to grips with the core problem of human language, which I take to be this: having mastered a language, one is able to understand an indefinite number of expressions that are new to one's experience, that bear no simple physical resemblance and are in no simple way analogous to the expressions that constitute one's linguistic experience; and one is able, with greater or less facility, to produce such expressions on an appropriate occasion, despite their novelty and independently of detectable stimulus configurations, and to be understood by other who share this still mysterious ability. The normal use of language is, in this sense, a creative activity. This creative aspect of normal language use is one fundamental factor that distinguishes human language from any known system of animal communication.

It is important to bear in mind that the creation of linguistic expressions that are novel but appropriate is the normal mode of language use. If some individual were to restrict himself largely to a definite set of linguistic patterns, to a set of habitual responses to stimulus configurations, or to 'analogies' in the sense of modern linguistics, we would regard him as mentally defective, as being less human than animal. He would immediately be set apart from normal humans by his inability to understand normal discourse, or to take part in it in the normal way – the normal way being innovative, free from control by external stimuli, and appropriate to new and ever-changing situations.

It is not a novel insight that human speech is distinguished by these qualities, though it is an insight that must be recaptured time and time again. With each advance in our understanding of the mechanisms of language, thought, and behavior, comes a tendency to believe that we have found the key to understanding man's apparently unique qualities of mind. These advances are real, but an honest appraisal will show, I think, that they are far from providing such a key. We do not understand, and for all we know, we may never come to understand what makes it possible for a normal human intelligence to use language as an instrument for the free expression of thought and feeling; or, for that matter, what qualities of mind are involved in the creative acts of intelligence that are characteristic, not unique and exceptional, in a truly human existence.

I think that this is an important fact to stress, not only for linguists and psychologists whose research centers on these issues, but, even more, for those who hope to learn something useful in their own work and thinking from research into language and thought. It is particularly important that the limitations of understanding be clear to those involved in teaching, in the universities, and even more important, in the schools. There are strong pressures to make use of new educational technology and to design curriculum and teaching methods in the light of the latest scientific advances. In itself, this is not objectionable. It is important, nevertheless, to remain alert to a very real danger: that new knowledge and technique will define the nature of what is taught and how it is taught, rather than contributing to the realization of educational goals that are set on other grounds and in other terms. Let me be concrete. Technique and even technology is available for rapid and efficient inculcation of skilled behavior, in language teaching, teaching of arithmetic, and other domains. There is, consequently, a real temptation to reconstruct curriculum in the terms defined by the new technology. And it is not too difficult to invent a rationale, making use of the concepts of 'controlling behavior', enhancing skills, and so on. Nor is it difficult to construct objective tests that are sure to demonstrate the effectiveness of such methods in reaching certain goals that are incorporated in these tests. But successes of this sort will not demonstrate that an important educational goal has been achieved. They will not demonstrate that it is important to concentrate on developing skilled behavior in the student. What little we know about human intelligence would at least suggest something quite different: that by diminishing the range and complexity of materials presented to the inquiring mind, by setting behavior in fixed patterns, these methods may harm and distort the normal development of creative abilities. I do not want to dwell on the matter. I am sure that any of you will be able to find examples from your own experience. It is perfectly proper to try to exploit genuine advances in knowledge, and within some given field of study, it is inevitable, and quite proper, that research should be directed by considerations of feasibility as well as considerations of ultimate significance. It is also highly likely, if not inevitable, that considerations of feasibility and significance will lead in divergent paths. For those who wish to apply the achievements of one discipline to the problems of another, it is important to make very clear the exact nature not only of what has been achieved, but equally important, the limitations of what has been achieved.

I mentioned a moment ago that the creative aspect of normal use of language is not a new discovery. It provides one important pillar for Descartes' theory of mind, for his study of the limits of mechanical explanation. The latter, in turn, provides one crucial element in the construction of the anti-authoritarian social and political philosophy of the enlightenment. And, in fact, there were even some efforts to found a theory of artistic creativity on the creative aspect of normal language use. Schlegel, for example, argues that poetry has a unique position among the arts, a fact illustrated, he claims, by the use of the term 'poetical' to refer to the element of creative imagination in any artistic effort, as distinct, say, from the term 'musical', which would be used metaphorically to refer to a sensual element. To explain this asymmetry, he observes that every mode of artistic expression makes use of a certain medium and that the medium of poetry – language – is unique in that language, as an expression of the human mind rather than a product of nature, is boundless in scope and is constructed on the basis of a recursive principle that permits each creation to serve as the basis for a new creative act. Hence the central position among the arts of the art forms whose medium is language.

The belief that language, with its inherent creative aspect, is a unique human possession did not go unchallenged, of course. One expositor of Cartesian philosophy, Antoine Le Grand, refers to the opinion 'of some people of the East Indies, who think that Apes and Baboons, which are with them in great numbers, are imbued with understanding, and that they can speak but will not for fear they should be employed, and set to work'. If there is a more serious argument in support of the claim that human language capacity is shared with other primates, then I am unaware of it. In fact, whatever evidence we do have seems to me to support the view that the ability to acquire and use language is a species-specific human capacity, that there are very deep and restrictive principles that determine the nature of human language and are rooted in the specific character of the human mind. Obviously arguments bearing on this hypothesis cannot be definitive or conclusive, but it appears to me, nevertheless, that even in the present stage of our knowledge, the evidence is not inconsiderable.

There are any number of questions that might lead one to undertake a study of language. Personally, I am intrigued, primarily, by the possibility of learning something, from the study of language, that will bring to light inherent properties of the human mind. We cannot now say anything particularly informative about the normal creative use of language in itself. But I think that we are slowly coming to understand the mechanisms that make possible this creative use of language, the use of language as an instrument of free thought and expression. Speaking again from a personal point of view, to me the most interesting aspects of contemporary work in grammar are the attempts to formulate principles of organization of language which, it is proposed, are universal reflections of properties of mind; and the attempt to show that on this assumption, certain facts about particular languages can be explained. Viewed in this way, linguistics is simply a part of human psychology: the field that seeks to determine the nature of human mental capacities and to study how these capacities are put to work. Many psychologists would reject a characterization of their discipline in these terms, but this reaction seems to me to indicate a serious inadequacy in their conception of psychology, rather than a defect in the formulation itself. In any event, it seems to me that these are proper terms in which to set the goals of contemporary linguistics, and to discuss its achievements and its failings.

I think it is now possible to make some fairly definite proposals about the organization of human language and to put them to empirical test. The theory of transformational-generative grammar, as it is evolving along diverse and sometimes conflicting paths, has put forth such proposals; and there has been, in the past few years, some very productive and suggestive work that attempts to refine and reconstruct these formulations of the processes and structures that underlie human language.

The theory of grammar is concerned with the question: what is the nature of a person's knowledge of his language, the knowledge that enables him to make use of language in the normal, creative fashion. A person who knows a language has mastered a system of rules that assigns sound and meaning in a definite way, for an infinite class of possible sentences. Each language thus consists (in part) of a certain pairing of sound and meaning over an infinite domain. Of course, the person who knows the language has no consciousness of having mastered these rules or of putting them to use, nor is there any reason to suppose that this knowledge of the rules of language can be brought to consciousness. Through introspection, a person may accumulate various kinds of evidence about the sound–meaning relation determined by the rules of the language that he has mastered; there is no reason to suppose that he can go much beyond this surface level of data so as to discover, through introspection, the underlying rules and principles that determine the relation of sound and meaning. Rather, to discover these rules and principles is a typical problem of science. We have a collection of data regarding sound–meaning correspondence, the form and interpretation of linguistic expressions, in various languages. We try to determine, for each language, a system of rules that will account for such data. More deeply, we try to establish the principles that govern the formation of such systems of rules for any human language.

The system of rules that specifies the sound–meaning relation for a given language can be called the 'grammar' – or, to use a more technical term, the 'generative grammar' – of this language. To say that a grammar 'generates' a certain set of structures is simply to say that it specifies this set in a precise way. In this sense, we may say that the grammar of a language generates an infinite set of 'structural descriptions', each structural description being an abstract object of some sort that determines a particular sound, a particular meaning, and whatever formal properties and configurations serve to mediate the relation between sound and meaning. For example, the grammar of English generates structural descriptions for the sentences I am now speaking; or, to take a simpler case for purposes illustration, the grammar of English would generate a structural description for each of these sentences:

(1) John is certain that Bill will leave.
(2) John is certain to leave.

Each of us has mastered and internally represented a system of grammar that assigns structural descriptions to these sentences; we use this knowledge, totally without awareness or even the possibility of awareness, in producing these sentences or understanding them when they are produced by others. The structural descriptions include a phonetic representation of the sentences and a specification of their meaning. In the case of the cited examples (1) and (2), the structural descriptions must convey roughly the following information: they must indicate that in the case of (1), a given psychological state (namely, being certain that Bill will leave) is attributed to John; whereas in the case of (2), a given logical property (namely, the property of being certain) is attributed to the proposition that John will leave. Despite the superficial similarity of form of these two sentences, the structural descriptions generated by the grammar must indicate that their meanings are very different: one attributes a psychological state to John, the other attributes a logical property to an abstract proposition. The second sentence might be paraphrased in a very different form:

(3) That John will leave is certain.

For the first there is no such paraphrase. In the paraphrase (3) the 'logical form' of (2) is expressed more directly, one might say. The grammatical relations in (2) and (3) are very similar, despite the difference of surface form; the grammatical relations in (1) and (2) are very different, despite the similarity of surface form. Such facts as these provide the starting point for an investigation of the grammatical structure of English; and more generally, for the investigation of the general properties of human language.

To carry the discussion of properties of language further, let me introduce the term 'surface structure' to refer to a representation of the phrases that constitute a linguistic expression and the categories to which these phrases belong. In the sentence (1), the phrases of the surface structure include: 'that Bill will leave', which is a full proposition; the noun phrases 'Bill' and 'John'; the verb phrases 'will leave' and 'is certain that Bill will leave', and so on. In the sentence (2), the surface structure includes the verb phrases 'to leave' and 'is certain to leave'; but the surface structure of (2) includes no proposition of the form 'John will leave', even though this proposition expresses part of the meaning of 'John is certain to leave', and appears as a phrase in the surface structure of its paraphrase, 'that John will leave is certain'. In this sense, surface structure does not necessarily provide an accurate indication of the structures and relations that determine the meaning of a sentence; in the case of sentence (2), 'John is certain to leave', the surface structure fails to indicate that the proposition 'John will leave' expresses a part of the meaning of the sentence; although in the other two examples that I gave the surface structure comes rather close to indicating the semantically significant relations.

Continuing, let me introduce the further technical term 'deep structure' to refer to a representation of the phrases that play a more central role in the semantic interpretation of a sentence. In the case of (1) and (3), the deep structure might not be very different from the surface structure. In the case of (2), the deep structure will be very different from the surface structure, in that it will include some such proposition as 'John will leave' and the predicate 'is certain' applied to this proposition, though nothing of the sort appears in the surface structure. In general, apart from the simplest examples, the surface structures of sentences are very different from their deep structures.

The grammar of English will generate, for each sentence, a deep structure, and will contain rules showing how this deep structure is related to a surface structure. The rules expressing the relation of deep and surface structure are called 'grammatical transformations'. Hence the term 'transformational-generative grammar'. In addition to rules defining deep structures, surface structures, and the relation between them, the grammar of English contains further rules that relate these 'syntactic objects' (namely, paired deep and surface structures) to phonetic representations on the one hand, and to representations of meaning on the other. A person who has acquired knowledge of English has internalized these rules and makes use of them when he understands or produces the sentences just given as examples, and an indefinite range of others.

Evidence in support of this approach is provided by the observation that interesting properties of English sentences can be explained directly in terms of the deep structures assigned to them. Thus consider once again the two sentences (1) 'John is certain that Bill will leave', and (2) 'John is certain to leave'. Recall that in the case of the first, the deep structure and surface structure are virtually identical, whereas in the case of the second, they are very different. Observe also that in the case of the first, there is a corresponding nominal phrase, namely, 'John's certainty that Bill will leave (surprised me)'; but in the case of the second, there is no corresponding nominal phrase. We cannot say 'John's certainty to leave surprised me'. The latter nominal phrase is intelligible, I suppose, but it is not well-formed in English. The speaker of English can easily make himself aware of this fact, though the reason for it will very likely escape him. This fact is a special case of a very general property of English: namely, nominal phrases exist corresponding to sentences that are very close in surface form to deep structure, but not corresponding to such sentences that are remote in surface form from deep structure. Thus 'John is certain that Bill will leave', being close in surface form to its deep structure, corresponds to the nominal phrase 'John's certainty that Bill will leave'; but there is no such phrase as 'John's certainty to leave' corresponding to 'John is certain to leave', which is remote from its deep structure.

The notions of 'closeness' and 'remoteness' can be made quite precise. When we have made them precise, we have an explanation for the fact that nominalizations exist in certain cases but not in others – though were they to exist in these other cases, they would often be perfectly intelligible. The explanation turns on the notion of deep structure: in effect, it states that nominalizations must reflect the properties of deep structure. There are many examples that illustrate this phenomenon. What is important is the evidence it provides in support of the view that deep structures which are often quite abstract exist and play a central role in the grammatical processes that we use in producing and interpreting sentences. Such facts, then, support the hypothesis that deep structures of the sort postulated in transformational generative grammar are real mental structures. These deep structures, along with the transformation rules that relate them to surface structure and the rules relating deep and surface structures to representations of sound and meaning, are the rules that have been mastered by the person who has learned a language. They constitute his knowledge of the language; they are put to use when he speaks and understands.

The examples I have given so far illustrate the role of deep structure in determining meaning, and show that even in very simple cases, the deep structure may be remote from the surface form. There is a great deal of evidence indicating that the phonetic form of a sentence is determined by its surface structure, by principles of an extremely interesting and intricate sort that I will not try to discuss here. From such evidence it is fair to conclude that surface structure determines phonetic form, and that the grammatical relations represented in deep structure are those that determine meaning. Furthermore, as already noted, there are certain grammatical processes, such as the process of nominalization, that can be stated only in terms of abstract deep structures.

The situation is complicated, however, by the fact that surface structure also plays a role in determining semantic interpretation.[1] The study of this question is one of the most controversial aspects of current work, and, in my opinion, likely to be one of the most fruitful. As an illustration, consider some of the properties of the present perfect aspect in English, for example, such sentences as: 'John has lived in Princeton'. An interesting and rarely noted feature of this aspect is that in such cases it carries the presupposition that the subject is alive. Thus it is proper for me to say: 'I have lived in Princeton' but, knowing that Einstein is dead, I would not say: 'Einstein has lived in Princeton'. Rather, I would say: 'Einstein lived in Princeton'. (As always, there are complications, but this is accurate as a first approximation.) But now consider active and passive forms with present perfect aspect. Knowing that John is dead and Bill alive, I can say: 'Bill has often been visited by John', but not 'John has often visited Bill'; rather, 'John

---

[1] I discuss this matter is some detail in 'Deep structure, surface structure and semantic interpretation', to appear in *Studies in general and oriental linguistics*, commemorative volume for Dr. Shiro Hattori, R. Jakobson and S. Kawamoto (eds.), Tec Corporation for Language and Educational Research, Tokyo, in press.

often visited Bill'. I can say: 'I have been taught physics by Einstein' but not 'Einstein has taught me physics'; rather, 'Einstein taught me physics'. In general, active and passive are synonymous and have essentially the same deep structures. But in these cases, active and passive forms differ in the presuppositions they express; put simply, the presupposition is that the person denoted by the surface subject is alive. In this respect, the surface structure contributes to the meaning of the sentence in that it is relevant to determining what is presupposed in the use of a sentence.

Carrying the matter further, observe that the situation is different when we have a conjoined subject. Thus given that Hilary is alive and Marco Polo dead, it is proper to say: 'Hilary has climbed Mt. Everest', but not 'Marco Polo has climbed Mt. Everest'; rather, again, 'Marco Polo climbed Mt. Everest'. (Again, I overlook certain subtleties and complications.) But now consider the sentence: 'Marco Polo and Hilary (among others) have climbed Mt. Everest'. In this case, there is no expressed presupposition that Marco Polo is alive, as there is none in the passive: 'Mt. Everest has been climbed by Marco Polo (among others)'.

Notice further that the situation changes considerably when we shift from the normal intonation, as in the cases I have just given, to an intonation contour that contains a contrastive or expressive stress. The effect of such intonation on presupposition is fairly complex. Let me illustrate with a simple case. Consider the sentence: 'the Yankees played the Red Sox in Boston'. With normal intonation, the point of main stress and highest pitch is the word 'Boston' and the sentence might be an answer to such questions as 'where did the Yankees play the Red Sox?' ('in Boston'); 'what did the Yankees do?' ('they played the Red Sox in Boston'); 'what happened?' ('the Yankees played the Red Sox in Boston'). But suppose that contrastive stress is placed on 'Red Sox', so that we have 'the Yankees played the RED SOX in Boston'. Now, the sentence can be the answer only to: 'who did the Yankees play in Boston'. Note that the sentence presupposes that the Yankees played someone in Boston; if there was no game at all, it is improper, not just false, to say: 'the Yankees played the RED SOX in Boston'. In contrast, if there was no game at all, it is false, but not improper, to say: 'the Yankees played the Red Sox in Boston', with normal intonation. Thus contrastive stress carries a presupposition in a sense in which normal intonation does not, though normal intonation also carries a presupposition in another sense; thus it would be improper to answer the question 'who played the Red Sox in Boston?' with 'the Yankees played the Red Sox in Boston' (normal intonation). The same property of contrastive stress is shown by the so-called cleft sentence construction. Thus the sentence: 'It was the YANKEES who played the Red Sox in Boston' has primary stress on 'Yankees,' and presupposes that someone played the Red Sox in Boston. The sentence is improper, not just false, if there was no game at all. These phenomena have generally been overlooked when the semantic role of contrastive stress has been noted.

To further illustrate the role of surface structure in determining meaning, consider such sentences as this: 'John is tall for a pygmy'. This sentence presupposes that John is a pygmy, and that pygmies tend to be short; hence given our knowledge of the Watusi, it would be anomalous to say: 'John is tall for a Watusi'. On the other hand, consider what happens when we insert the word 'even' in the sentence. Inserting it before 'John' we derive: 'even John is tall for a pygmy'. Again, the presupposition is that John is a pygmy and that pygmies are short. But consider: 'John is tall even for a pygmy'. This presupposes that pygmies are tall; it is therefore a strange sentence, given our knowledge of the facts, as compared, say, to 'John is tall even for a Watusi', which is quite all right. The point is that the position of 'even' in the sentence 'John is tall for a pygmy' determines the presupposition with respect to the average height of pygmies.

But the placement of the word 'even' is a matter of surface structure. We can see this from the fact that the word 'even' can appear in association with phrases that do not have any representation at the level of deep structure: consider for example, the sentence 'John isn't certain to leave at 10; in fact, he isn't even certain to leave at all'. Here, the word 'even' is associated with 'certain to leave', a phrase which, as noted earlier, does not appear at the level of deep structure. Hence in this case as well properties of surface structure play a role in determining what is presupposed by a certain sentence.

The role of surface structure in determining meaning is illustrated once again by the phenomenon of pronominalization.[2] Thus if I say 'each of the men hates his brothers', the word 'his' may refer to one of the men; but if I say 'the men each hate his brothers', the word 'his' must refer to some other person, not otherwise referred to in the sentence. However, the evidence is strong that 'each of the men' and 'the men each' derive from the same deep structure. Similarly, it has been noted that placement of stress plays an important role in determining pronominal reference. Consider the following discourse: 'John washed the car; I was afraid someone ELSE would do it'. The sentence implies that I hoped that John would wash the car, and I'm happy that he did. But now consider the following: 'John washed the car; I was AFRAID someone else would do it.' With stress on 'afraid', the sentence implies that I hoped that John would not wash the car. The reference of 'someone else' is different in the two cases. There are many other examples that illustrate the role of surface structure in determining pronominal reference.

───────

[2] The examples that follow are due to Ray Dougherty, Adrian Akmajian and Ray Jackendoff. See Chomsky, *ibid.*, for references.

To complicate matters still further, deep structure too plays a role in determining pronominal reference. Thus consider the sentence 'John appeared to Bill to like him'. Here, the pronoun 'him' may refer to Bill but not John. Compare: 'John appealed to Bill to like him'. Here, the pronoun may refer to John but not Bill. Thus we can say 'John appealed to Mary to like him', but not 'John appeared to Mary to like him', where 'him' refers to 'John'; on the other hand, we can say 'John appeared to Mary to like her', but not 'John appealed to Mary to like her', where 'her' refers to Mary. Similarly, in 'John appealed to Bill to like himself', the reflexive refers to Bill; but in 'John appeared to Bill to like himself', it refers to John. These sentences are approximately the same in surface structure; it is the differences in deep structure that determine the pronominal reference.

Hence pronominal reference depends on both deep and surface structure. A person who knows English has mastered a system of rules which make use of properties of deep and surface structure in determining pronominal reference. Again, he cannot discover these rules by introspection. In fact, these rules are still unknown, though some of their properties are clear.

To summarize: the generative grammar of a language specifies an infinite set of structural descriptions, each of which contains a deep structure, a surface structure, a phonetic representation, a semantic representation, and other formal structures. The rules relating deep and surface structure – the so-called 'grammatical transformations' – have been investigated in some detail, and are fairly well understood. The rules that relate surface structure and phonetic representation are also reasonably well-understood (though I do not want to imply that the matter is beyond dispute; far from it). It seems that both deep and surface structure enter into the determination of meaning. Deep structure provides the grammatical relations of predication, modification, and so on, that enter into the determination of meaning. On the other hand, it appears that matters of focus and presupposition, topic and comment, the scope of logical elements, and pronominal reference, are determined, in part at least, by surface structure. The rules that relate syntactic structures to representations of meaning are not at all well understood. In fact, the notion 'representation of meaning' or 'semantic representation' is itself highly controversial. It is not clear at all that it is possible to distinguish sharply between the contribution of grammar to the determination of meaning, and the contribution of so-called 'pragmatic considerations', questions of fact and belief and context of utterance. It is perhaps worth mentioning that rather similar questions can be raised about the notion 'phonetic representation'. Although the latter is one of the best established and least controversial notions of linguistic theory, we can, nevertheless, raise the question whether or not it is a legitimate abstraction, whether a deeper understanding of the use of language might not show that factors that go beyond grammatical structure enter into the determination of perceptual representations and physical form in an inextricable fashion, and cannot be separated, without distortion, from the formal rules that interpret surface structure as phonetic form.

So far, the study of language has progressed on the basis of a certain abstraction: namely, we abstract away from conditions of use of language and consider formal structures and the formal operations that relate them. Among these formal structures are those of syntax, namely, deep and surface structures; and also the phonetic and semantic representations, which we take to be certain formal objects related to syntactic structures by certain well-defined operations. This process of abstraction is in no way illegitimate, but one must understand that it expresses a point of view, a hypothesis about the nature of mind, that is not *a priori* obvious. It expresses the working hypothesis that we can proceed with the study of 'knowledge of language' – what is often called 'linguistic competence' – in abstraction from the problems of how language is used. The working hypothesis is justified by the success that is achieved when it is adopted. A great deal has been learned about the mechanisms of language, and, I would say, about the nature of mind, on the basis of this hypothesis. But we must be aware that in part, at least, this approach to language is forced upon us by the fact that our concepts fail us when we try to study the use of language. We are reduced to platitudes, or to observations which, though perhaps quite interesting, do not lend themselves to systematic study by means of the intellectual tools presently available to us. On the other hand, we can bring to the study of formal structures and their relations a wealth of experience and understanding. It may be that at this point we are facing a problem of conflict between significance and feasibility, a conflict of the sort that I mentioned earlier in this talk. I do not believe that this is the case, but it is possible. I feel fairly confident that the abstraction to the study of formal mechanisms of language is appropriate; my confidence arises from the fact that many quite elegant results have been achieved on the basis of this abstraction. Still, caution is in order. It may be that the next great advance in the study of language will require the forging of new intellectual tools that permit us to bring into consideration a variety of questions that have been cast into the waste-bin of 'pragmatics', so that we could proceed to study questions that we know how to formulate in an intelligible fashion.

As noted, I think that the abstraction to linguistic competence is legitimate. To go further, I believe that the inability of modern psychology to come to grips with the problems of human intelligence is in part, at least, a result of its unwillingness to undertake the study of abstract structures and mechanisms of mind. Notice that the approach to linguistic structure that I have been outlining has a highly traditional flavor to it. I think it is no distortion to say that this approach makes precise a point of view that was inherent in the very important work of the 17th and 18th century universal grammarians, and that was developed, in various ways, in rationalist and romantic philosophy of language and mind. The approach deviates in many ways from a more modern, and in my opinion quite erroneous conception that knowledge of language can be accounted for as a system of habits, or in terms of stimulus–response connections, principles of 'analogy' and 'generalization', and other notions that have been explored in 20th century linguistics and psychology, and that develop from traditional empiricist speculation. The fatal inadequacy of all such approaches, I believe, results from their unwillingness to undertake the abstract study of linguistic competence. Had the physical sciences limited themselves by similar methodological strictures, we would still be in the era of Babylonian astronomy.

One traditional concept that has re-emerged in current work is that of 'universal grammar', and I want to conclude by saying just a word about this topic. There are two kinds of evidence suggesting that deep-seated formal conditions are satisfied by the grammars of all languages. The first kind of evidence is provided by the study of a wide range of languages. In attempting to construct generative grammars for languages of widely varied kinds, investigators have repeatedly been led to rather similar assumptions as to the form and organization of such generative systems. But a more persuasive kind of evidence bearing on universal grammar is provided by the study of a single language. It may at first seem paradoxical that the intensive study of a single language should provide evidence regarding universal grammar, but a little thought about the matter shows that this is a very natural consequence.

To see this, consider the problem of determining the mental capacities that make language acquisition possible. If the study of grammar – of linguistic competence – involves an abstraction from language use, then the study of the mental capacities that make acquisition of grammar possible involves a further, second order abstraction. I see no fault in this. We may formulate the problem as the problem of determining the intrinsic characteristics of a device of unknown properties that accepts as 'input' the kind of data available to the child learning his first language, and produces as 'output' the generative grammar of that language. The 'output', in this case, is the internally represented grammar, mastery of which constitutes knowledge of the language. If we undertake to study the intrinsic structure of a language-acquisition device without dogma or prejudice, we arrive at conclusions which, though of course only tentative, still seem to me both significant and reasonably well-founded. We must attribute to this device enough structure so that the grammar can be constructed within the empirically given constraints of time and available data, and we must meet the empirical condition that different speakers of the same language, with somewhat different experience and training, nevertheless acquire grammars that are remarkably similar, as we can determine from the ease with which they communicate and the correspondences among them in the interpretation of new sentences. It is immediately obvious that the data available to the child are quite limited – the number of seconds in his lifetime is trivially small as compared with the range of sentences that he can immediately understand and can produce in the appropriate manner. Having some knowledge of the characteristics of the acquired grammars and the limitations on the available data, we can formulate quite reasonable and fairly strong empirical hypotheses regarding the internal structure of the language-acquisition device that constructs the postulated grammars from the given data. When we study this question in detail, we are, I believe, led to attribute to the device a very rich system of constraints on the form of a possible grammar; otherwise, it is impossible to explain how children come to construct grammars of the kind that seem empirically adequate under the given conditions of time and access to data. But if we assume, furthermore, that children are not genetically predisposed to learn one rather than another language, then the conclusions we reach regarding the language-acquisition device are conclusions regarding universal grammar. These conclusions can be falsified by showing that they fail to account for the construction of grammars of other languages, for example. And these conclusions are further verified if they serve to explain facts about other languages. This line of argument seems to me very reasonable in a general way, and when pursued in detail it leads us to strong empirical hypotheses concerning universal grammar, even from the study of a particular language.

I have discussed an approach to the study of language that takes this study to be a branch of theoretical human psychology. Its goal is to exhibit and clarify the mental capacities that make it possible for a human to learn and use a language. As far as we know, these capacities are unique to man, and have no significant analogue in any other organism. If the conclusions of this research are anywhere near correct, then humans must be endowed with a very rich and explicit set of mental attributes that determine a specific form of language on the basis of very slight and rather degenerate data. Furthermore, they make use of the mentally represented language in a highly creative way, constrained by its rules but free to express new thoughts that relate to past experience or present sensations only in a remote and abstract fashion. If this is correct, there is no hope in the study of the 'control' of human behavior by stimulus conditions, schedules of reinforcement, establishment of habit structures, patterns of behavior, and so on. Of course, one can design a restricted environment in which such control and such patterns can be demonstrated, but there is no reason to suppose that any more is learned about the range of human

potentialities by such methods than would be learned by observing humans in a prison or an army – or in many a school-
room. The essential properties of the human mind will always
escape such investigation. And if I can be pardoned a final
'non-professional' comment, I am very happy with this outcome.

ABRAHAM KAPLAN

The life of dialogue

DR. ABRAHAM KAPLAN *came to the United States from Odessa, Russia, in 1923 and became a citizen in 1930. The son of a Rabbi, Dr. Kaplan spent a portion of his youth in Minnesota as a student at Duluth Junior College and the College of St. Thomas, St. Paul, where he graduated with a B.A. in 1937. In 1942 he received his Ph.D. from the University of California, Los Angeles.*

He has been on the faculties of the University of California and the University of Michigan. He has been a visiting professor at Harvard University, Columbia University, Hebrew Union College, and the University of Cincinnati. His ability in the classroom was recently cited by TIME *when he was named one of the ten greatest college professors in America.*

At the present time, Dr. Kaplan is on leave to the University of Hawaii, Honolulu, directing the Fifth East-West Philosophers' Conference.

Honors awarded him include a Guggenheim Fellowship; Rockefeller Fellowship; a Fellow of the Center for Advanced Study of Behavioral Sciences, Palo Alto, California; an honorary degree from the University of Judaism (a seminary); named the Adolf Meyer Lecturer of the American Psychiatric Association in 1964; a Fellow of the Western Behavioral Sciences Center, La Jolla, California; and the president of the American Philosophical Association (Pacific Division).

He was written four major books and is a member of the Board of Editors of the Journal of Applied Behavioral Science (Washington, D.C.). He served in a similar editorial capacity for three international publications in the field of philosophy.

Dr. Kaplan is a member of numerous learned and professional societies and associations.

Being reminded of my youth in the world of debate very much tempts me to begin: 'Mr. Chairman, Worthy Opponents, Honorable Judges, Ladies and Gentlemen'. It has a sweet, old-fashioned ring, does it not? The people we talk to nowadays are so seldom regarded as being worthy and honorable.

I suppose it is true after all that it is impossible to go home again. Being back here in Minnesota, and especially listening to the scientific papers, I recall that my undergraduate days were occupied with science; I took my degree in chemistry. I envy my fellow panelists their opportunity for scientific objectivity. Increasingly through the years I have moved away from the objectivity of science to what I must say is now a frankly subjective point of view. Although my topic is 'Communication', and although I will be referring quite often to the ideas of Martin Buber (the philosopher and theologian who taught at the Hebrew University in Jerusalem until his death just a few years ago), in fact I will not be talking about these objective matters but about something quite subjective. The French writer Anatole France, in commenting on the inevitable subjectivity of literary criticism, said that if a critic were really honest, he would say to his audiences something like this: 'Ladies and gentlemen, I am going to talk to you about myself on the subject of Shakespeare'. Let me say that I am going to talk to you about myself on the subject of communication; maybe, a little more broadly, not only about myself, but also about you; about this concrete human situation at just this moment and in just this place.

Yesterday we heard about a great many fascinating people.

We heard not only about the birds and the bees, frustrated tree crickets and frightened chimpanzees, but also about autistic children, abandoned children, and illegitimate children; people who were sensorially deprived and culturally deprived; pygmies and Watusis, Yankees and Red Sox. But we did not address ourselves concretely and specifically to the people that *we* are here and now. It seems to me that this was not an incidental feature of the scientific approach to language and communication; it is quite characteristic of the part that is played by these ideas in contemporary philosophy, at least in the English speaking world.

In philosophy there has been an interesting movement in the conceptualization of the problems of this field, a movement which – as so often is true of philosophy, alas! – is in just the reverse direction of what has been happening in linguistics and related scientific disciplines. Philosophy some three or four decades ago was extremely structural in its approach, extremely formal. It gradually moved from considerations of logical syntax to the field of semantics, and recently has been occupied with the uses and functions of language, at just a time when, as Chomsky pointed out, the linguist abstracts from the uses and functions of language to focus on structural descriptions. I believe that there is another step yet to be taken, not as an alternative, by any means, to the formal, abstract, structural approach but, – as Chomsky himself emphasized – as a very much needed supplement to that approach, if we are going to interest ourselves in the human needs which communication serves. That step is to look, not at the medium of communication nor at the conditions – neurological or environmental or whatever – which make communication possible, but to look at the human beings who are communicating with one another, and to ask, what happens to people when they communicate?

I want to approach this question in terms of a basic category of Martin Buber's thinking, no doubt familiar to many of you, concerning two modalities of human relationship: the 'I-Thou' modality and the 'I-It' modality. Roughly speaking, in the first modality both we and the other accept ourselves as the human beings that we are; in the second modality we dehumanize, depersonalize the other and in the process also dehumanize, depersonalize ourselves.

Most philosophy today is carried on in the I-It modality. There is even a curious idiom which we have taken over from Britain – people talk of 'doing' philosophy, as though there is some process to which certain impersonal materials are subjected – to what end, serving what values, expressing what human needs is very hard to say. How different this is from the approach to philosophy of a Socrates, or, for that matter, of an Isaiah: 'Come, let us reason together'! Most philosophy today, Buber has said, is monologue. The philosopher is not talking to anyone, not even to his colleagues. He may be talking *for* them; he wants them to hear what he is saying. But it is not a genuine saying – there is no one at the other end, or, at any rate, no one wholly human in that kind of communication.

This style of philosophizing – as I proceed I shall suggest that it is a style found throughout our culture – is associated with certain conceptions of the nature of language and communication. The philosopher does something in his own peculiar way, then he projects his personal peculiarities onto the cosmos – he uses language in a certain way, then concludes that this is the very essence of language. The ideal language, especially for the philosophical analyst, has become more and more a language which is dehumanized and depersonalized. Many analysts look to scientific discourse, especially in its most mathematical forms. To do the scientist justice, I think we would have to say that it is not really scientific discourse the philosopher is looking at, but the philosopher's own picture, usually a distorted one, of scientific discourse. Finally, what is held up to us as a paradigm is the language we use to communicate with machines.

I would like to make something quite clear at the outset. I am a warm admirer of technology, and warmly appreciate both what has already been achieved and the great promise I see for the future, in the application of new technologies to the tasks of education. I think we have scarcely begun to exploit the potentialities of the teaching machine and of other such devices. But Chomsky was a thousand times right when he warned that there is a great danger in this development, namely, that we let the technology determine our values rather than the other way round.

I sometimes think that maybe somebody should devote some effort to the design and construction of *learning* machines; in the mass universities of the future I foresee a possibility of great lecture halls with a teaching machine at one end and a bank of learning machines at the other end, in a closed circuit, while somewhere in a small room a few human beings sit and talk, educating one another. There are two quite different processes which can go on in the schooling situation; both are types of communication, I suppose. One I call *instruction*, the transmission of information and of certain skills in the processing of that information and in the handling of other materials. There is another process for which I reserve the term *education;* it is a process of human growth, and can take place only when human beings are fully interacting with one another. I believe that instruction can be carried out by machine, probably better than it can be done by humans; and I believe that whatever *can* be done by machine *should* be done by machine, so as to leave the human being free to devote himself to what is most distinctively human.

There is a danger in this point of view also, and I am anxious not to be misunderstood. The danger is that the insistence on the human values which technology is to serve may become an excuse for hostility to the whole scientific enterprise, to the intellect, to reason, to the human mind. There is a danger of obscurantism here, and I want to dissociate myself from obscurantism as strongly as I can. I do not believe in the two cultures of which C.P. Snow speaks – science on one side and the humanities on the other. Science is itself one of the greatest and the most distinctively human of man's achievements. Buber makes the point in this way, that in differentiating the modalities of the Thou and the It he is not condemning the domain of the It nor the I–It modality. He says, on the contrary, 'You cannot hold onto life without It, its reliability sustains you. But should you die in It, your grave would be in nothingness'. More simply, 'Without It man cannot live, but with It alone he can not live as a man'.

I want to look at communication, then, not in terms of the It alone, but in terms of the ways in which communication can bring human beings together or hold them apart – or, at any rate, bring them together not as human beings but as depersonalized objects to one another.

I believe that a great deal of communication in modern society is of this second kind. There is an enormous amount of talk in our society, an enormous amount of communication, I suppose, written as well as spoken; but in another sense there is really very little communication, very little that is actually being said. It may be, as Augenstein put it, that the mind is the last sanctuary of individuality and integrity. I begin to wonder if even the mind is a sanctuary, because it is increasingly being invaded by communications which say nothing to us, which mean nothing to us, but which nevertheless take hold of us, compel our attention, and make it harder than it is already to see clearly ourselves, other people, and the world around us. Apparently our society is coming increasingly to have a horror of silence. Wherever we go nowadays someone is dinning something into our ears; whether it is in a market, an elevator, an airplane, at a restaurant, or for that matter, in a school room. If it isn't talk we must listen to, then it is somebody's notion of music, or something else to fill the perceptual void. Is it this same horror of being sensorially deprived of which we were told yesterday, I wonder?

At the same time there is in our society the most exaggerated conception of what can be accomplished by talk, both for good and for ill. We think that if only the right things are said, somehow all will be well. We are probably the greatest masters of euphemism the world has ever known. We also fear that if the wrong things are said, the foundations of society will totter. I have never been able to understand why in so many communities there is so much anxiety about the kinds of speakers who are invited to a campus. The man comes, and however outrageous his views are, he talks for an hour or two and goes his way; but I talk to the students day after day, week after week, and month after month, and when at the end of the semester I read the final exams I see I've had no effect whatever. Charlie Brown once called Lucy a name, and she said to him, 'Sticks and stones may break my bones, but names will never hurt me – you blockhead!' We worry about violence on television screens, but we are not so much worried, apparently, about the violence in the real world around us – in our own cities, in Vietnam, in the Middle East. We want to protect our children from the symbol rather than from the reality; the symbol comes to be more real to us than the reality itself. I suppose that there is a whole generation now for whom the cosmos and space have taken on reality only because we've seen it on TV. In our time, that is the final authentication.

We pay an enormous price for this belief in magic. Magic always exacts an enormous price; more accurately, it is reality that takes its revenge on us for closing our eyes to it. Part of the price we pay, I believe, is what is variously called alienation, the crisis of identity, and such like. I believe that one resaon –

one only but a significant reason – for the rise of the demonstration as a social phenomenon, whether on campuses or on city streets, is connected with this alienation. The demonstrator is saying, 'Look at me as a human being, listen to me, and talk *to* me, not *at* me. Let us establish communication; this is what I am demanding above all else'.

In so many institutions, not just educational institutions but pervasively in our society, this human need which we all know and feel deeply is more and more being denied. Aristotle wrote a treatise on ethics in which two whole chapters were devoted to the subject of friendship. He says, 'Even if a man had all other goods, if he had no friends life would not be worth living'. I doubt if a single book on ethics written in English in the twentieth century so much as contains the word 'friendship' in the index, except possibly as an example of an abstract noun. So far as our general social patterns are concerned, we do not have friends; we have contacts, connections, clients, customers, or constituents. (Why these words all begin with 'C' Chomsky might explain!)

We even formulate some of our technological aims in just this perspective. Augenstein spoke of 'human engineering'. There are some real and important problems dealt with under that rubric; I do not want to derogate their importance. But I also want to call attention to how easy – I almost said 'natural' but I think it is quite unnatural – how easy it is for us to see a person as material to be shaped or as an instrumentality to be used, rather than as a human being. Real life, Martin Buber once said, is meeting. It is a certain kind of relationship in which the humanity of those relating is absolutely central.

What bearing does this have on the communication process? Let me put it this way. There is a certain kind of communication which we all know, very precious to us, very different from the kinds of communication which are most common and which are most commonly analyzed. I would like to propose a distinctive label for it. Let me call it 'communion' instead of communication.

The model that has been built up for the usual kind of communication is a very valuable model for many purposes; let me insist upon that. It is roughly as follows. There is a source of possible messages, each of which can be conceived as the result of certain choices from among the set of alternatives that can be selected for transmission. The choices are made with linked probabilities, not altogether independent of one another; the materials are suitably encoded and fed into a channel where they are transmitted to a receiver, having been distorted in certain respects by the noise in the channel; they are then decoded, more or less accurately; finally, someone takes the decoded message and goes his way. Notice that in this process the human beings appear only at the termini; everything else of interest takes place in between.

In what I am calling communion the relationship between the human beings is a direct one. It is unmediated; it is as though the human beings are put directly into contact with one another. (In fact, we use such idioms as 'Keep in touch with me'.) Although in a strict sense there are, of course, many mediating processes, somehow they do not have the significance in communion which they have in communication. Consider what happens when you are experiencing grief, and a friend puts his arm around you. (Charlie Brown asks somewhere whatever happened to the good, old-fashioned, arms-around-the-shoulder sympathy which he never gets.) No words are exchanged and they aren't needed, but there is something important which relates the two people in that situation. Or, you look at someone whom you know, or whom you would like to know, and your eyes meet. The eyes are the window of the soul, as are the hands, the lips – everything with which we can communicate. When the eyes meet, it is not that something which lies between the two people connects them, but as though two human beings, for those brief moments, have become just one. Eye contact is a very intimate relationship; were you to catch the eye of a stranger and hold it, in our culture at least, either the contact would be broken very quickly or the relationship would move to a new plane – whether of hostility or of something quite other, I do not know. But it would not remain where it was; you are not the same again after what has passed between you. Yet it is not so much that something has passed between you, but that in that moment you were truly *with* one another as human beings.

There are many human relationships which manifest *reciprocity* – I do something for you, you do something for me. Quite often it would be more accurate to say, 'I do something *to* you, and in return I allow *you* to do something to me'. This is a very different kind of relationship than a *mutual* one, in which we do something together which neither of us can do separately. Mutuality does not involve our depersonalizing each other, but exactly the contrary; it allows each to become even more fully human. There is a difference after all, is there not, between talking *with* someone and talking *to* them or, in that suggestive idiom, talking *at* them.

There is a kind of communication distinct from both monologue and dialogue for which I propose the term *duologue*. In duologue there are two people talking, but they are not talking with one another. Duologue is not communion in the present sense; it is a kind of communication. Information is being transmitted, but not to human beings; at any rate, there are not two human beings at the same time. The mark of duologue is that the two people are not really together in mutuality; they are at best only in a reciprocal relationship. While one person is talking, the other one is not listening; he is only thinking of what he will say when it is his turn to talk. The cocktail party is the institutionalization of duologue, and so, I am afraid, is the classroom. First the professor talks and the students don't listen; then the students talk or write and the professor doesn't listen or read; at any rate, they are not human beings talking *with* one another. Each is doing something *to* the other, while he claims that he is doing something *for* the other, although it is never quite clear who is doing what for whom.

What is most characteristic of communion is that feature of language which Marler called 'openness', and which Chomsky described as creative, or as governed by a transformational generative grammar. I would put it in layman's terms in this way. When people are in communion, when they are in this narrow sense really communicating with one another, the content of what is being communicated does not exist prior to and independently of that particular context. There is no message, except in a *post-hoc* reconstruction, which is fixed and complete beforehand. If I am really talking with you, I *have* nothing to say; what I say arises as you and I genuinely relate to one another. I do not know beforehand *who* I will be, because I am open to you just as you are open to me. This, I think, is what makes growth possible among human beings, and why it seems to me impossible really to teach unless you are learning; why you cannot really talk unless you are listening. You are listening not only to the other, you are listening to yourself. Indeed, in a fundamental sense – I would even say in quite a literal sense – self and other are now so intertwined that we need new conceptual frameworks, new categories to describe what is happening.

Chomsky said that in his view the study of language is a branch of theoretical psychology. That seems to me to be very much in the right direction. I should want also to insist that it must be a social psychology. Perhaps we should say that the study of language is really a branch of theoretical sociology, as Marler put it. A certain kind of social structure or a certain pattern of involvement of several organisms is essential to communication. Buber says that we become human beings only insofar as we enter into this special relationship with other human beings; through the *Thou* a man becomes an *I*. I caught something very like this in the invocation which Dr. Carlson delivered: 'We need each other to become ourselves'. We need talk, not merely to fill a sensory vacuum, but to fill what would otherwise be a far more intolerable void within ourselves, where we seek an identity.

Just as there is a difference between communion and communication, between I–Thou and I–It, there is a corresponding difference between a self which is truly human and a self which is only an object among other objects – an It in the domain of the It. This is the difference between an *identity* and an *identification*. We all have plenty of identifications. They are not only easy to come by, they are impossible to avoid. Everywhere you turn, you are given another identification, another number. The identity is something quite different. It is not what allows us to be located in the domain of the It. Our identity is what makes us the particular persons that we are.

I do not know if we can speak of a 'breakdown' of communication. Perhaps it would be more accurate to speak of the failure to achieve communication – I do not know whether we have ever had it; I do not believe in the myth of a Golden Age. This failure, then, truly to communicate with one another is very much bound up with the search for identity. That search has been a task for the young ever since there were young. But the failure of communication, I believe, is also bound up with great social problems both on the domestic and the foreign scene. More and more people seem to be coping with their problems by adopting negative identities, thinking to find themselves by differentiating themselves from the other, to become selves not by being *with* the other, but by being against the other. Racism, both black and white, has, I think, this psychodynamic. 'I can't talk with you; indeed, I won't talk with

you. Only in that refusal can I be myself'. In the Rabbinic
tradition there is a beautiful aphorism which runs, 'If I am I
only because you are you, and you are you only because I am I,
then I am not I and you are not you'. For then we face one
another only as two mirrors endlessly reflecting their emptiness
into one another.

I am sure that if you heard it yesterday, the line of Augenstein's is still with you – the deeply moving line, 'Little George,
it's important to me that you are who you are.' That is perhaps
the greatest thing which any human being can say to any other
human being. It is important to me that you are who you are,
and that I am who I am; you and I together can communicate
with each other, and thereby more fully realize all the potentialities for the human which lie within us.

Such ideas have quite a history in modern times. The socio-
logist and philosopher, George Herbert Mead, is especially
associated with the theory of an intimate relationship between
the development of the self and the use of what he calls 'significant symbols'. In Mead this fundamental dialogue with the
'generalized other' takes place within the self. Moreover, the
self is analyzed in Mead as though it comes to be once for all.
We pay a lot of attention to the infant at just the stage when
he is learning to talk, and we imagine that once he has learned
how to talk he has acquired a self; the rest is no longer of any
particular concern to us. We leave off, it seems to me, at precisely
the point where we should begin. The self comes to be in every
dialogue; it is generated in every act of communication. I am
other than I was because of what I am now saying to you. If
I am really saying it to you, if you are *with* me in this act of
communication, you also are now other than you previously
were.

People can be together, in various senses of that term,
without really being *with* one another, just as they can talk
without really communicating. Buber calls this kind of together-

ness a *collectivity* and he contrasts it with a *community*. A community is an aggregation in which there is a binding of human beings to one another; in a collectivity, he says, there is no binding together, only a bundling together. We *use* one another in the collectivity. We may say 'we', but this is a kind of group egotism. It has no genuine content, any more than the word 'I' has a genuine content when the man who speaks it has no identity and truly does not know who he is; it may be he has not yet become an 'I'. So also in our social aggregations we too often have not yet become a community.

The question may be asked whether it is possible to establish communion between two people with absolutely opposing ideas.

It seems to me that unless we can establish communion in these cases, we will not have communion at all. It is easy to talk with people we love; the trick is to be able to talk with people we do not love. Alas, we must even learn to live in a world of hate. Only, I should like to say that ideas can differ from one another without opposing one another. I am a relativist; I do believe that values are objective, but I also believe that they can be objective and at the same time plural. I think there is too great a tendency for us to suppose that all values can be linearly ordered. We too often assume that there is a single dimension of values, so that if you consider any two different values, one must be better and the other worse. We recognize that this is not so in the arts; it makes no sense to ask whether Keats was a better poet than Chopin was a composer. That's just idle talk; what we want to do is to appreciate the poetry and also appreciate the music. There are many kinds of poetry even, and for that matter, many different kinds of sonnets, and so on. In the house of our Lord there are indeed many mansions. We can absolutely oppose another only when we close ourselves off from the other. My thesis has been that when we do that, we are closing ourselves off from ourselves as well. I think I would have to say that if two people are absolute in their opposition to one another, they have both abandoned their humanity; it is not possible for human beings absolutely to oppose one another. The same point could be put in this way, that loving is intrinsic to our human nature. As soon as we begin to see *them* as no longer human, we ourselves become increasingly involved in inhumanities. I would say, therefore, that it *is* possible to establish communion between people with opposing ideas. It can be done just insofar as we abandon our absolute stance, and are prepared really to talk with the other. I think of a concrete political case which is very meaningful to me. The problems today in the Middle East can be regarded as being in a significant degree problems of instituting dialogue. There is an apocryphal story that an American Undersecretary recently exclaimed in the United Nations, 'Why can't Israel and her Arab neighbors settle their differences like Christian gentlemen?' It is said that a Buddhist who overheard him remarked, 'The trouble is, that's just what they're doing!'

Many people who talk about the problems of our cities are victims again of a myth of the Golden Age. They speak of the 'breakdown of the community', as though somewhere, in the past, people really were together, and now we have lost it all; usually the loss is blamed on technology or science or numbers or something modern. All that, I think, is a myth; but I do think it is true that a great deal of our lives with other people is spent in collectivities and not in communities. Recently someone proposed what I think is a brilliant numerical measure of the degree of civilization of any society: the number of strangers whom you can trust, or, as I would prefer to say in this context, the number of strangers whom you can talk to, whom you can talk with, whom you can understand and know that they understand you. This, of course, is another way of saying that you enter into community with them.

It is one of the features of our time, I am afraid, that we can talk with strangers only in times of disaster. Last night when we were snowbound or thought we might be – I confess, I *hoped* we might be – there was a little electricity in the air, so it seemed to me, a little movement away from the I-It to the I-Thou, a little softening, a little humanizing of one another. This effect was observed in the power black-out in New York, and earlier during the Blitz in London. What a pass we have come to, if we can allow ourselves our humanity only when there is some chance that we will pay for it with our lives! Instead, we pay with our lives the rest of the time, with the kind of lives we lead – what Thoreau called lives of quiet desperation. Perhaps in our time they are not so quiet, but they are just as desperate. Unless we talk with one another, we deny ourselves our humanity in the very moment when we turn aside from the humanity of the other.

To what can we attribute the withholding of self? Is it a lack of mutual trust? If I had to answer in brief, I probably could not do better than with the one word 'fear'. Fear of mutuality operates on several different levels. There is fear of rejection; there is fear of acceptance, which may betray my inadequacy; there is fear of being accepted and proving adequate, but then finding myself committed. There may also be fear for the very integrity of the self. If I open myself to you, I may be swallowed; if I give myself to you, there may be nothing left of me. There is, I think, a basic dilemma of identity: I need the other for my identity, but the other is at the same time a threat to my identity. The dilemma might be put in this way: How can I be what I am without fear of being different from you, and how can I be *with* you without fear of losing my identity? I do not think that such dilemmas have solutions: we only learn to cope with them, and go on to the next.

There are some profoundly moral and religious implications in all this, which Buber made explicit. No doubt many of you have already been drawing out these implications. One might distinguish between two kinds of evil in human experience.

One is that in which the It predominates in our lives – not that the It itself is evil, but the domination of the It is evil. This is the kind of evil in which we do not communicate with others; we only manipulate others. We keep them in the domain of the It. This violates a principle of Kantian morality to be found in many versions in Christianity, in Judaism, and in other world religions. It is the evil which consists in treating other human beings only as means to ends, and not experiencing them as ends in themselves. There is a second kind of evil, much harder to see, intimately bound up with the first. That is the evil in which we talk, but only to ourselves. It is the evil, not of living in the domain of the It, but of mistaking I for Thou. We worship, but we worship only idols of our own making, and become, as the Psalmist rightly pointed out, like the idols we ourselves have made.

A central problem of religious thought can be formulated as a problem in communication. It is expressed in the cry, 'Why art Thou silent?' Why does not God give me a sign? How shall I reach Him? Why does He turn away from me?' Quite extraordinary, is it not, how these same locutions might be used to express our sense of alienation from other human beings. If only we can establish communication! Every Thou, in Martin Buber's idiom, is a glimpse of the eternal Thou. The religious experience is an intensification of the experience which we have in every encounter in which we are truly with the other and experience the other as Thou.

In that case, Buber concludes – and I think quite rightly – God talks to man all the time. He talks to man in all the things and all the beings which He sends to man; man answers in all his dealings with these things and beings. We can answer in two different ways – it is the same contrast which I have been drawing on all along. Buber finds these two responses symbolized in the two Scriptural characters of Adam and Abraham. God called to Adam, 'Where art thou?' and Adam ran and hid. But God said, 'Abraham, Abraham', and he answered, 'Here I am!', thereby instituting the dialogue which established the Biblical religion.

There are some very popular words today – cliches, in fact: 'encounter', 'confrontation', and (I will be the first to admit it) 'dialogue'. These three words have a very interesting property – you can combine them in any order and sound as though you are really 'with it'. 'We have entered upon this confrontation so as to make possible a dialogue which will lead to a genuinely human encounter'. Or, 'We have entered upon this dialogue so that the encounter. . .' You can work out the variations. I believe that these words have become cliches because what they are pointing to, in however vague and confused a way, is something universal, and universally important to us.

I want to conclude by injecting one other element into an already complicated situation. The aim of all communication, it seems to me, is to arrive at communion. To put it more boldly, the aim of all talk is to pave the way for silence. In all talk we move from silence to silence. Only, there are two very different kinds of silence. There is the silence of hostility, of ignorance, of bewilderment; the silence which means that I have nothing to say to you nor you to me. There is the very different silence of understanding, of love, of knowledge, where the situation is not that we have nothing to say to each other, but that nothing more needs to be said. What we really need, I think – I invite my scientific colleagues to look at this problem – is a syntax of silence. We might do well to focus on the ways in which human beings communicate when they are not using language, or its conventional equivalents in gesture and the like.

A psychiatrist friend in Los Angeles told me once of the following experience. Late one night he was at the Los Angeles General Hospital and had occasion to go to the surgical waiting room. There was only one person there, a woman who was sobbing as though her heart would break. He asked the nurse on duty who it was. She said, 'That is Mrs. Gonzales; her husband has just died on the operating table'. He said, 'Oh, I know the case'. He went over and sat down by her, and said, 'Mrs. Gonzales, I am Dr. Ingham. It happens that I knew about your husband's case. He had the best of care; I know the surgeon. He would have died very shortly in any case...' and he went on. As he talked, her crying subsided, and was replaced by a few whimpers; then she quieted down and was even able to smile a little through her tears, as she held his hand. He sat and talked with her for some time, then looked at his watch and realized he had to leave. As he was walking out the nurse on duty called him over and said, 'Dr. Ingham, I didn't know that you spoke Spanish'. 'Spanish! I don't know any Spanish'. She said, 'Well, then, what were you talking about with Mrs. Gonzales? She doesn't know a word of English'. That really was talk, real communication, was it not?

There is a need to become aware of and develop the use of nonverbal expressions for more meaningful intra- and inter-personal relationships. But man has an unlimited capacity for perversion. We can turn everything to an evil purpose, misuse every instrumentality. It is quite true that in many of the examples I gave of real communication or communion, I turned to the nonverbal. But the nonverbal also can become a device for not being with others, but on the contrary, for holding people apart. Consider, for instance, the falsely hearty handshake, or my favorite example, what I call the 'stewardess syndrome.' (I recently lectured on 'Loneliness' and discussed the stewardess syndrome at some length. After the lecture, among the people who came up to talk with me was one very attractive young woman who looked vaguely familiar; she said, 'I was the stewardess on your flight to. . .!') I do think that nonverbal methods of communication can be used very much more, but this use would only shift the problem. Let me also make clear, in the other direction, that I did not mean to imply that words always keep people apart; words can also serve to bring people together.

I think that in our schools, at any rate, there is altogether too little silence. Everbody in the school situation seems to panic at the thought that maybe someone will be sitting without talking or listening to talk, and without even reading or writing. We have our students carefully read Walt Whitman, and perhaps even parse his lines about loafing and inviting the soul, but we do not allow them to do it. If you are on the faculty, you cannot invite your soul because you have a committee meeting; if you are a student it is because you have an assignment to read, a paper to write. It may be that, not only in our schools but throughout our society, if we talked less, we might say more; if we did not try so hard to communicate, we might be able to commune. If we did not search so hard for our own identities, but occupied ourselves with the other, we might find what we were not seeking. If we listen, it may be that we will be able at last to respond, 'Here I am!'

The impulse to escape is always present. This is the impulse in all of us to turn away from the real world which presents problems that sometimes seem overwhelming, and to turn instead to a fantasy world of our own making, where we can solve problems without effort. 'The mind is its own place, and in itself can make a hell of heaven and a heaven of hell.' I see a good deal of this turning away from reality. I think that is the significance of the use of drugs in our time; and there are other escape mechanisms operative. But I don't think anything is gained by closing the door for escape, or by putting heavier shackles on our prisoners. Men try to escape from reality when they find the reality painful and feel powerless to do anything about it. What we need to do is to address ourselves to what is producing the pain, and to the fact as well as the feeling of powerlessness. This seems to me to be as true with regard to the problems of the ghetto as it is with regard to the problems of student unrest – as it is, indeed, with regard to the problems of war and peace on the world scene. Of course, the reality is painful, and, of course, our powers are limited, and of course, the problems are almost insoluble. But there is a world of salvation in the word 'almost'. At any rate, there is a world of hope in that 'almost', and perhaps that is all – or almost all – that a man can ask for.

ERIC H. LENNEBERG

A word between us

DR. ERIC H. LENNEBERG *was born in Germany and attended high school in Rio de Janeiro, Brazil, and after graduation spent seven years in business in that country. He joined the United States Army in 1945 and served for two years. After discharge he became a United States citizen while attending the University of Chicago where he earned a B.S. in 1949. It was the beginning of his specialized education which included an M.A. in linguistics in 1951 and a Ph.D. in psychology and linguistics at Harvard University in 1956.*

He became a post-doctoral fellow in medical sciences specializing in neurosciences at the Harvard Medical School and completed those studies in 1958. For one year he was at the Massachusetts General Hospital, Neurological Service, as a Resident Fellow. It was after this that he went to MIT as a Research Associate in biophysics communication while serving as assistant professor of psychology at the Harvard Medical School and Children's Hospital.

In 1964, he was on leave for a year to the University of Zurich as a visiting professor of psychology. Immediately prior to assuming his present position at Cornell University in 1968, he was with the University of Michigan as Professor of Psychology and a Fellow in the Center for Human Growth and Development.

His professional affiliations include membership in the Linguistic Society of America, American Psychological Association, Society for Research in Child Development, and a Fellow of the American Association for the Advancement of Science.

What is Language? (I)

There is nothing obvious about the nature and function of language. The discovery of its nature is as difficult as an attempt to see our own retina or to sense the motion of the planet under our feet. Linguists have been accused by students of animal behavior that they are complicating the picture unduly by the introduction of formalization and by creating an aura of philosophy about language that is – they claim – unnecessary and merely serves to becloud the straightforward and 'simple' facts. R. A. and B. T. Gardner, for instance, state (unpublished ms):

> The theories [on language] that can be
> constructed are never as interesting as
> the natural phenomena themselves, and
> the gathering of data is a self-justifying
> activity.

They find that 'careful scholarship' concerning the extent to which another species might be able to use human language is a less efficient approach towards elucidation of the nature of language than their own 'alternative approach [namely] to try to teach a form of human language to an animal'.

But suppose we could show that what is being taught to the animal only bears some tenuous and farfetched similarity to language, or that it is actually quite different in the most essential aspects; would that not make the 'gathering of data' a rather futile undertaking? As it turns out, it *is* possible to characterize language – to zero in on the question: what is language? – and, having done this, we do in fact discover that there is no evidence that the Gardners are teaching another species the use of human language.

It is a pity that the social and biological sciences are so prejudiced against theory. It is actually impossible to gather data without at least an implicit theory; and if such a theory were always made explicit, the data gathering would no longer appear as an end in itself but as something that is secondary to theoretical formulations.

The first step towards an appreciation of the nature of language is an inventory of what is and what is not biologically essential to language communication. I shall say there is language communication between two individuals as long as (1) there is substantial agreement between the two concerning the semantic interpretation of most sentences produced by either of them; *and* if (2) these sentences may be judged by an independent speech community to be based upon a natural language such as English, or Turkish, or Navaho.

Condition (1) holds if it can be demonstrated that both individuals assign the same truth-value to a sentence that is a proposition (e.g., 'the sun is shining today'); or that both individuals would give the same answer to a question concerning an easily verifiable matter of fact (e.g., 'is the hat on the table?'); or if both agree on the behavior demanded by an imperative (e.g., 'take the shoe from the bed!'), etc. Note that in many instances, although we suspect that language communication between two individuals is taking place, it cannot be demonstrated (e.g., in a prisoner who refuses to talk to his interrogator).

Condition (2) purposely is formulated quite liberally. 'Based upon. . .' does not mean that it must be acoustically transmitted or that a given writing system must be adhered to. Finger-spelling, Morse-code transmission, or semaphore may all be based upon English. A production system is based upon a natural language if there is an isomorphism between bona fide utterances in a given language and the products of the system.[1] Where such an isomorphism is lacking, the products of the system usually are degradations (of varying degree) from the natural language.

With these definitions in mind, we may now ask what is the most essential condition that makes language communication possible. We shall start by investigating language communication between human beings because we have so much empirical evidence here, but we shall not prejudge the possibility that language communication between different species is demonstrable. However, we shall presently specify the nature of the evidence necessary to compel us to admit that cross-species language communication has taken place.

When we survey language communication in man, we soon discover that the skills of hearing and seeing are not essential. Congenitally deaf individuals become proficient language communicators through the use of writing or finger-spelling. (In the latter, every letter of a word can be shown by a specific hand-signal, although some words are usually abbreviated and represented by a single sign. Thus isomorphism on a word level is fairly well preserved.) Congenitally blind children learn to speak without undue difficulties; no one has ever doubted a blind person's capacity for language communication.

The study of children with cleft palates and other oral or laryngeal impediments has made it abundantly clear that man's language communication is also not dependent upon the existence of articulatory skills. It is perfectly possible in individuals who cannot make intelligible sounds (Lenneberg 1962), which may be demonstrated by the methods discussed below.

What, then, are the prerequisites in man for language communication? We cannot demonstrate language communication

---

[1] More accurately: if for every element in language L there is a corresponding element in the invented communication system S such that one can be mapped onto the other, and if every operation in L is preserved in S.

(as defined above) in babies six months of age or younger. Also, training and exposure to language are definitely less efficient during the first year of life than during the third year. Thus we may suspect that a certain degree of maturation of the brain is a prerequisite.

Further, we know that the lack of proper exposure to language communication will block language development, and therefore we may confidently assert that a certain 'treatment' of the growing individual is another prerequisite. The treatment consists of *speaking to the child*, where the word *speaking* need not be taken literally. The deaf and blind Helen Keller began to develop a capacity for language communication as soon as a tactual signal system could be developed and thus a channel opened through which exposure to language was possible.

I have shown elsewhere (Lenneberg 1967) that there is reasonable evidence to make us suspect that exposure to language must take place during a limited number of years (from age 2 to 12, the period during which the brain goes through its last stages of physical maturation). The observations available so far suggest that under the influence of language exposure, the brain is modified in specific ways during these formative years, making language communication possible. If the appropriate environmental influences are lacking during this period, the child seems to outgrow the time of plasticity, so that a belated exposure may be of little use for the acquisition of language capacities.

There is a wealth of further evidence to indicate that the crucial factor that makes language communication possible is to be found in an as yet difficult-to-specify aspect of brain physiology. Language disturbances consequent upon specific brain lesions have been studied since the middle of the nineteenth century. The capacity for language communication may be totally or subtotally abolished by destruction of brain tissue while the patient's other mental functions continue to operate fairly satisfactorily. This condition is called aphasia. However, it has not been widely recognized that aphasic symptoms are merely an extreme degree of disturbances that are quite common in their milder form and that occur in a wide spectrum of situations in which the physiological functions of the brain are slightly affected either by drugs, toxic substances, or systemic disease and its pathophysiology. In fact, anything that causes stress may alter brain functions in a mild way, producing slight irregularities that may interfere with language communication. The individual cannot think of the right word at the right time; his articulation may become slurred; stammering may occur; he may begin to speak too much and without finishing anything, and thus become incoherent; or he may show an inability to understand what is being said to him. There are only few symptoms of aphasia that do not have correlates in the language of a person with transient alterations of his normal physiological brain function.[2] (However, many abnormal events in the brain leave language unaffected, and not all failures in language communication are due to abnormal physiology; nor is it possible yet to make accurate predictions about the correlation of clinical speech problems and pathological events.)

All of these considerations point to the same conclusion: the most important factor for language communication is located in the brain and has to do with its peculiar function. This may not be a very startling conclusion, but when we put the data together, we find that there is much that is not always recognized and is, in fact, far from obvious.

First of all, we find that there must be some rather specific aspects to human brain function that make language communication possible. This is so because language can be *affected* specifically. The power of learning new facts, for instance, is

---

[2] Telegraphic, belabored style is one such exception.

relatively independent of language capacity. Aphasic adults and speechless children may acquire a great deal of knowledge, even though some aspect of their brain function is insufficient for language communication. On the other hand, some feeble-minded children may exhibit some simple forms of language communication but have marked impairment in learning. Chimpanzees give various signs of intelligence and an ability to make associations or to comprehend complex situations, but they do not develop language comprehension from mere exposure to language communication as does a child without a tongue (one such case has been fully documented by Dr. James Bosma of the National Institutes of Health). Language, therefore, does not appear to be simply a huge repertoire of associations (a fact that is also brought into question by the ability of the congenitally blind to acquire language). Nor is it simply a consequence of great intelligence. (The relation that exists is more subtle than can be reported here; see Lenneberg 1967.)

Secondly, the possibility of localization of certain language functions in the brain attests that there are rather specific specializations for this activity. But one must not conclude from this that these functions are individual skills that reside in given tissues such as Broca's area or the angular gyrus. Rather, the functions underlying language communication are integrated activities involving an intricate net of structures, all functionally interrelated, the activity of one modulating the activity of the other.

Parenthetic remarks on cognition

Despite the relative specificity of language functions, we must recognize their intimate relation to cognitive function and to the physiological processes underlying cognition. Therefore, the nature of the claims made here will be better understood if seen in the light of a more general theory of cognition.

We find vastly different types of animals living in essentially the same physical environment. Yet they do not seem to perceive the same things in the same ways. The divergences cannot be explained simply by differences in peripheral mechanisms, especially sensory thresholds. There is substantial overlap in the auditory and visual thresholds of many mammals, but differences in their brain function cause a different behavioral reaction to what is potentially available to their senses. Ethological research of the last few decades makes it plausible to assume that different brains process physical data in different fashions. One species may treat a set of configurations as essentially similar where another species reacts as if there were irreconcilable differences. These interspecies differences are not very obvious if the stimulus material consists of man-made patterns that do not occur freely in the natural environment (triangles, stripes, geometric forms, etc.). But as soon as different species are confronted with more natural 'stimulus textures', the animals' reactions become dramatically different. Little systematic work has been done along these lines, and our impressions are still based on uncontrolled observations made in the field on unrestrained animals. An exception are the cybernetic studies made by European scholars under the leadership, especially, of E. v. Holst. Even though there is a relative scarcity of experimental data, the conclusion seems safe that different types of brains are associated with different cognitive processes, and that types of cognition are species specific.

Let us focus for a moment on one aspect of cognition: pattern recognition. What are the main features of a device that must recognize some given constellation in the natural environment? For illustrative purposes, we might take an imaginary prosthetic device built for the blind: a portable apparatus that makes one noise when approaching an obstacle and a different noise when brought close to a step-down. The task of this sort of machine is relatively simple – much simpler than most of the recognition tasks solved by animals with quite primitive brains. But even here it becomes obvious that the device cannot be a simple transducer; it must do much more than translate directly, i.e., point by point, its input to some output. It cannot, for instance, transfer light and dark to high and low pitch; we want it to accept as input an infinity of patterns (all the different configurations one sees when walking through streets) but make only three responses (e.g., obstacle, step, safe-walking). Thus the task is one of sorting out or categorizing input. Now, how can the infinitely variable input be processed? The incoming patterns cannot just be passed through a stable bank of templates or filters, because the device would then lack versatility and would make mistakes whenever the patterns in the scanned environment failed to conform to certain rigid specifications. Instead, the machine would have to be sensitive to certain relations that remain constant amidst continuously varying factors – it would have to extract in variances from an everchanging world. A machine equipped to behave in this way would, in short, be a kind of computer; the processes intervening between input and output would be computations.

Formally, pattern recognition in animals is no less a computational process than what goes on in artifacts of the sort described. This position is a modern version of a mechanistic point of view. We no longer believe that we can characterize a brain as a mechanical device, but we are still committed to the idea that its operations are based on the same laws of nature that constitute the subject matter of the natural sciences. We are as adamant today as our forerunners were a hundred years ago, that brain function should not be explained by postulation of 'vital' forces that are different from those encountered in physics and chemistry. However, the modern version of the mechanistic point of view is more modest in its hopes for actual achievements. We do not expect to be able to give definitive explanations, and we are fully prepared to produce knowledge that continues to be bounded by ignorance. The brain-machines that we postulate are 'soft' devices, and the computations they perform are the result of biochemical action that sets the stage for neurophysiological processes.

Our attempts to construct formalisms that describe the gross behavior of brains – our attempts to offer mathematics for the biological events – must not be mistaken for theories on the function of the machines properly speaking. They are no more than descriptions, that is, attempts to systematize scattered observations.

Now let me say a word on the types of computations that may be postulated for brains and their associated cognitive process: recognition. The recognition capacity with respect to a linear stimulus continuum such as light or sound has different degrees of coarseness for different species. This is the same as to assert that animals have different *differential* thresholds. What is a just-noticeable-difference (j.n.d.) for the Tasmanian skink, may be a set of colors containing 10 j.n.d.'s for the spotted kangaroo. Imagine three animals with the same absolute thresholds – but one has a very coarse perception, another less coarse, the third a very fine one. The animal whose j.n.d. interval is the same as the absolute threshold can tell only presence vs. absence of stimulation – for instance, a violet color looks the same as a red color. It can perceive all the stimuli (an infinitely large number) within the limits of its threshold, but it can never tell one color apart from any other. The animal whose j.n.d. interval is smaller, say a little narrower than the gamut of the animal's absolute threshold, can tell apart only highly contrasting colors. Thus this animal can tell stimulation vs. no-stimulation and low stimuli from high stimuli; it sees two *different* colors but only *two* different ones, even though it is sensitive to an infinity of light stimuli. Finally, there is the animal whose absolute thresh-

old is the same as those of the first two described, but whose
j.n.d. interval is so small that it may recognize a large number
of different stimuli. In no case, however, will there ever be an
animal that sees or, in general, perceives *all* the differences that
nature provides *objectively*. No animal could possibly be so
constructed as to see differences in the number of molecules of
two masses, or have a specific taste sensation for every molecular structure. Perception in organisms must always be a
many-to-one mapping. Recently the topologists Zeeman and
Buneman (1968) have formulated the mathematical concept
tolerance for the type of mappings involved here. Without going
into details, their concept conveys the notion that organisms
are tolerant with respect to the stimuli they respond to; they
admit of variations in the stimuli and thus emit a given response
to a gamut of conditions.

When an organism responds, it manifests a change in its
activity. The most general and, in a sense, simplest type of
response is the *perception* of some differences (notice that I
think of perception, itself, as a response), i.e., the behavior
of neurons in the brain changes from state S to state S1 at a
time when a condition in the organism's environment changes
from Y to Z. We may say that the computer, *brain*, performs in
this instance an operation: it computes the relationship Y to Z.
The organism takes note of the difference between Y and Z, and
this manifests itself as the transition from S to S1.

The relationships that are being computed even by relatively primitive brains are much more complex than ascertaining
simple differences. The stimulus patterns surrounding animals
are not linear continua, and the simplest vertebrates (and a
great many invertebrates) give evidence of having a fairly
complex repertoire of operations at their disposal with which
to compute intricate relationships.

In short, what is important in this discussion is (1) that cognition is species specific (which, of course, does not claim

that the types of cognition of different kinds of animals are unrelated to one another); and (2) that at least recognition and pattern perception must be viewed as a system of relational computations.

What is language? (II)

Even a superficial examination of language communication suggests that its proper function is predicated upon the proper function of cognition, including recognition. We have seen in part I that language can hardly be regarded as a collection of associations, a stockpile of individual items where all that is needed for speaking is the acquisition of one item after another. It becomes clearer now that language in all of its phases is a process or a mode of dealing with potential information in the environment, a peculiar way of processing data. The learning of a language does not involve the tagging of a particular thing but the selection of a set of principles for doing relational computations upon the environment. The child who was asked what a hole was, answered characteristically, 'A hole is to dig'. In other words, a hole is not that one unique stimulus configuration in the child's backyard, but is anything upon which a given relational calculus produces an invariant result. The computer that can assign a specific response to all 'hole-configurations' must be equipped to carry out a number of operations resulting in fairly specific relational computations. If we admit that brains with their associated cognitive processes are species specific, we must also admit that it is quite likely that there will be many types of brains that are not endowed with the requisite capacities to carry out those operations necessary to categorize stimulus configurations into holes vs. non-holes. This assertion does not imply that there might not be some stimulus configurations recognizable by means of relational computations that are quite within the capacities of a wide range of animals.

Virtually every aspect of language, including everything in semantics, syntax, and phonology, is a reflection of relational computations performed by our brain upon the objective world. Any one of the natural languages reflects only a small part of the relational computations that the human brain is capable of, and a person who speaks Gururu natively is not restricted to the relational computations that are reflected in his language (as has been claimed occasionally; see Whorf 1956). When a child acquires the language of his surroundings, he learns that certain computations available to him by virtue of having a human brain are labeled either by words or by syntactic means. We say that he understands a word or sentence when he gives evidence that the word can cause the computer – his brain – to go through a certain routine of relational computations. What I am proposing here is that the repertoire of relational computations is the same for all human brains; that a natural language is a system of tags (alas, fairly sloppy ones) for a certain number of modes of relational computations; and that during acquisition of a natural language, the child learns just which computational processes are being tagged.

Just as there is in sensory perception, to use Zeeman's term, a certain *tolerance* on the set of perceivable points (j.n.d. intervals), there appears to be a certain tolerance in natural languages on the exactness of the computational processes that are being tagged by a word. Therefore, it is difficult to say exactly what the necessary and sufficient relations are that categorize a certain stimulus configuration such as *table* or *house* or *red*. Language communication is quite efficient, despite a lack of perfect agreement on just what relations are in question. This is best demonstrated by the process of metaphorizing, which is so characteristic of all natural languages, as well as the use that people make of languages. *Table* is usually the result of relational computations concerning flatness, squareness, proportions, and positions such that one can sit *at* the object (i.e., a certain relationship to the human figure), etc. However, these computations are not rigidly fixed in number and nature. Speakers may extend the meaning of the word, make creative use of it, without danger of being incomprehensible to other speakers of the same language. If I were to speak of a table-mountain, or if I were to state that John shares his table but not his bed with Mary, any speaker of English would have an idea of what I meant, even though I would have taken liberties with common usage. It is exactly this tolerance for groups of relations that are being computed in the semantic process that accounts for the fluidity of languages and their relatively quick change in the course of history.

The study of language communication across species

I would now like to address myself to the challenge of the Gardners (unpublished ms) and their claim that they are teaching a form of human language to a chimpanzee through the medium of what they call the American Sign Language. I assume that the experiment is being conducted to demonstrate aspects of chimpanzee capacities that are (a) new to us, and (b) have some relevance to human communication via natural languages. In other words, the Gardners are not trying to confirm further that animals, including chimpanzees, can perform acts upon verbal commands such as 'heel', 'sit', 'go', etc. Nor do we need experimental data to show that chimpanzees can learn to perform gestures, or that chimpanzees, dogs, or cats will do things spontaneously to achieve an end, including certain tricks they have been trained to perform. Thus, the only question on which there is serious disagreement, and a question that must be settled by careful empirical demonstration, is the extent to which the animal may be trained to do something that resembles language communication among men. When I say *resemble*, I do not mean some far-fetched analogy based on utterly superficial similarities or on logical rather than biological similarities (such as, respectively, the speech of the parrot or the language of the honey bee). In order to show empirically that the chimpanzee trained by the Gardners is acquiring even a primitive aspect of language, five distinct demonstrations are necessary.

(1) A test of the language itself (as used from man to man). We have developed many communication systems that have very little to do with natural languages. For instance, the green-red traffic signals are not a simplified language; nor are the pantomimes that I may invent in a game of charades.

As noted, the Gardners report that they are using for their experiment the American Sign Language of the deaf. Those congenitally deaf persons in America who use sign language actually make use of three different systems: first, finger-spelling, in which every letter of a word is spelled out; second, a system of standardized shorthand signs for entire words; third, non-standardized, spontaneously created pantomime. When the deaf communicate, they tend to mix all three, though the third system serves more as vignettes to what they are saying (somewhat like our own use of gestures as we talk). In most casual conversations, the first and second systems are intermixed freely; when the subject matter is fairly technical, finger-spelling predominates; but even in light and familiar interchange, finger-spelling continues to be used.

The communication system that is being taught to the chimpanzee is apparently a mixture of the second and third systems; it differs from the communication of the deaf in an important way: there is no finger-spelling whatever. Thus we should first of all discover, what are the capacities of the communication system itself, and what is the proficiency of the trainers in communicating among each other. We would like to know what type of message can be sent, how much detail is preserved in the transmission, what is the mistake rate, etc. To answer these questions, the following experimental paradigm is indicated: two individuals must communicate with each other by signing, one asking questions, the other one answering them. In order to make sure that communication is not helped along by extraneous factors, two additional persons are needed as observers. The first person writes a question on a slip of paper that is handed to the second, who reads it and then translates it into hand signals. The third person sees the hand-signalled question and answers it, again by means of hand signals; the fourth person can only see the third; he does not know what has been asked, but writes on a slip of paper what the answer is. The written questions and answers remain as permanent records and constitute the data from which one may judge the efficiency and versatility of the communication system.

(2) A test of communication efficiency between man and chimpanzee. If test 1 has been shown to be successful in at least one circumscribed area (cf. also tests 4 and 5, below), we may examine communication across species. The experimental set-up must be the same as described for the first test, and would be run in the following way. One man would ask the question in writing; a second translate it into signs; a third watch the second and record in writing what he thinks is being signalled to the chimp; and a fourth watch the chimp and describe his reaction in writing (this man would not know what was actually being said to the animal). It would be a good precaution to send a signal to the fourth man at conclusion of the communication sent by number two; this would insure that the random behavior of a restless animal (who might blindly go through his acquired list of tricks) is not recorded as a response to a question or command.

(3) A test of the animal's knowledge of language. A parrot utters words, but all serious zoologists are agreed that the bird does not know any aspect of the language in which these words occur. Mention of the word *know* or *knowledge* need not scare the empiricist. There are objective, behavioral means of demonstrating the existence of knowledge of a language. They consist of limiting our test to question that may be answered by a yes–no gesture or to instructions that must be followed by appropriate behavior. Now, it is absolutely essential that both questions and instructions be phrased in sentences, however simple in construction and vocabulary, because the sentence (syntax) is the most characteristic aspect of language. There are no natural languages without syntax, and if even the most primitive syntax were unteachable, we could not agree that what has been taught is language-like. In the absence of syntax we would be back to single-word commands, such as 'come', 'paw', etc., which we already know animals can follow and which do not indicate language capacity (just as the jumping over a hurdle upon hearing a buzzer is not an analogue to word acquisition).

Notice that the crucial questions we should like to have answered by the experiment is whether and what the animal can *understand*. The only gestures that the animal need be required to emit are *yes* and *no* – two items of productive vocabulary! Thus, our stipulation is considerably more modest than what the Gardner's ape is at present required to do. All of the animal's spontaneous productions should be disregarded in our attempts to assess its *knowledge* of language. This is necessary in order to avoid fooling ourselves in a way similar to that caused by the horse, Clever Hans, and his owner, v. Osten. If we consider the animal's spontaneous productions and assess the appropriateness of these 'messages', we are simply testing our own ingenuity to assign interpretations to productions that might, for all we know, have been emitted randomly. It would always be possible to claim that the ape had 'intended' to tell us something – the dream it had last night or a thought that crossed its mind (probably concentrated on all sorts of monkey-business).

(4) A demonstration of the existence of simple language – operations. Naturally, we must use a very simple language, consisting of items that have meaning to the animal in his present environment. On the other hand, we must be sure that at least some of the basic aspects of every language are preserved. To guide us in our construction of the language to be taught, we should include only words or aspects that either are, or potentially could be, present in all languages of the world. At the same time, we should use only items and aspects of language that can be mastered by children in their very early stages of language development. This assures the construction of a truly primitive level of language comprehension. Following is a representative list of items that fulfill these demands. The total number is in fact considerably smaller than the productive vocabulary reported for the Gardners' animal.

Five object words:
   hat, shoe, table, window, bed.
Three action words:
   put, take, point.
Three qualifiers:
   small, big, black.
Five words indicating position or direction:
   on – up – high,[3] under – down – low,[3] from – out,[3] to – at,[3] with.
Four function words:
   no – not,[3] yes, and, is?[4]

---

[3] I.e., one word with this meaning.
[4] Signal for question.

The total vocabulary of the language need not consist of more than twenty words. The syntax need not consist of more than a single, basic construction used in either the imperative or the interrogative. For instance, 'Take [the] big shoe and put [it] under [the] bed!' or 'Is [the] big shoe under [the] bed?' This language is extremely primitive, and since we do not require the learner to speak it – only to understand it – even a highly retarded child could manage it.

The number of items and rules is kept here to an absolute minimum, but I consider their nature to be so representative of natural language that any substantial qualitative changes (such as elimination of prepositions or predication) would simply comprise the claim that 'a form of human language' is being used. What would remain would be a serious degradation of language communication – not just a primitivization.

(5) A test of productivity. Even though the subject is not expected to learn to 'say' (or sign) more than *yes* or *no*, we would have to require that his understanding is *productive.* By this I mean that it is not enough that he learns to answer a small number of stereotyped questions or to execute a few stereotyped commands. The learner must be able to answer essentially any question that is possible within this limited language or to execute any command that can be phrased with the few words. Further, his semantics, too, must be productive. The words *hat* and *table*, *big* and *small*, *on* and *under* must be understood in essentially all those contexts in which they are understood by the speakers of a natural language, and the mistakes that occur in understanding should be somewhat comparable to those committed by children. (Since the latter are difficult to assess in any objective way, we must be prepared to tolerate fairly broad deviations.)

As soon as the Gardners submit objective evidence on the positive performance of these five tests, I shall admit that the capacity for language acquisition is common to man and chimpanzee, and that man's superior achievements differ only quantitatively, not qualitatively from those of other primates (or at least the genus *Pan*).

A word between us

The series of tests above should reveal whether a given subject – human or animal – can discover the intricate net of relationships that underly the meaning of words and whether he can also identify the relationships between these relationships, that is, the syntactic connections between words. The subject will experience great difficulties with this task unless he tends to do with his environment (i.e., unless he cognizes the environment) as members of our species do when recognizing objects around them. Languages merely select from among those computations that the human mind performs when interacting with our surroundings. The word between us is the instrument by which it is possible to bring about accord of computations in different minds; but this can only be achieved if there is a propensity for making just these kinds of computations, of seeing these relationships among the heterogeneities called 'the environment'. The acquisition of words does not create a propensity for specific computations out of nothing. Teaching a child the meaning of a word does not introduce into his mind a mental operation the way a desk calculator would introduce computing facilities into an empty office. The speech community can do no more than say, 'Here is a word W; its correct usage requires the application of a given set of relational principles (computations) upon certain aspects of your milieu; find out for yourself how we use the word.' In short, the word between us is an incentive to select from among a range of computations, all of them from the general repertoire of computations for which our brain with its cognitive functions has been built by nature. Whether the brain of a chimpanzee has the same or similar propensities must yet be demonstrated. It is possible, but not probable (Lenneberg, in press).

As an appendix, I wish to draw attention to three common but erroneous views on the essentials of language.

(1) It is sometimes thought that an animal approaches man's language capacity to the degree that it acquires a large vocabulary – the more words the closer to man's language. But a language is not a simple store of items; it is a mode of operation. Even if a subject knew the meaning of four thousand isolated words, he would not know the language unless he understood some principles of syntax and some of the subtleties of usage pertaining to each word. The number of items learned is quite irrelevant to language capacity.

(2) Those of us who believe that language has a specific biological foundation are frequently misunderstood; our claim is not based on man's capacity to articulate or perceive auditorily but on his capacity to process potentially available information in the environment in highly specific ways. The biological foundation must be sought in the physiological processes underlying man's cognition. From this it should also be obvious that a belief in a biological foundation is *not an anti-environmental* position. Influences from the environment play an indispensable role in the new theory.

(3) Finally, it is sometimes claimed that a capacity for generative grammar has been demonstrated simply by showing that the subject is concatenating various items. Actually, this demonstrates very little. The word *generative* in grammar does not refer to the production or making of sentences. It is used as an abstract metaphor and denotes *principles that account for something*. For instance, Peano's five postulates could be said to 'generate' arithmetic sentences such as $3 + 2 = 5$; or the concept of the *a priori* generates a rational epistemology. The

principle of random selection might generate a table of random numbers. When the word – output of an organism or a machine is evaluated, we would like to know what the principles are that underly the production. In the case of a parrot, there *is* a generative principle (replication of some stereotyped phrase); but this principle is different from those that underly sentence formation of an adult speaker. In short, generativeness in grammar is not synonymous with 'combining of words'.

References

Gardner, R. A. and B. T. Gardner, 1968. Teaching sign language to a chimpanzee. (Unpublished manuscript.).

Lenneberg, E. H., 1962. Understanding language without ability to speak. *J. abnorm. soc. Psychol.* 65, 419–425.

Lenneberg, E. H., 1967. *Biological Foundations of Language*. New York, John Wiley.

Lenneberg, E. H., in press. On explaining language, *Science*.

Whorf, B. L., 1956. *Language, thought and reality* (J. B. Carroll, ed.), Cambridge, Mass., Technology Press of MIT, and New York, John Wiley and Sons, Inc.

Zeeman, E. C. and O. P. Buneman, 1968. Tolerance spaces and the brain, in *Towards a theoretical biology: an I.U.B.S. Symposium* (C. H. Waddington, ed.), Chicago, Aldine.

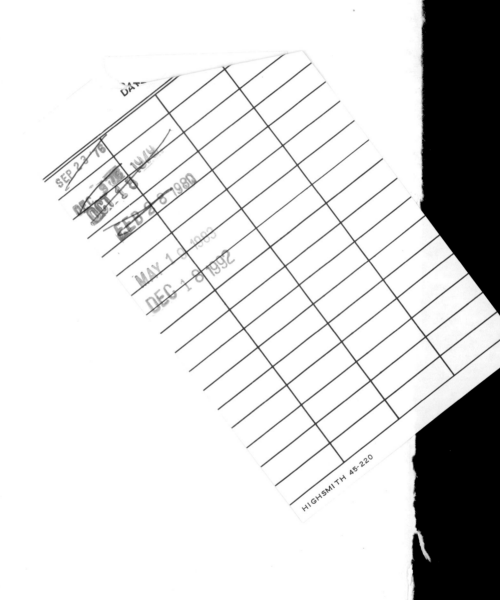